ORGANIZED

LIVING

ORGANIZED LIVING

DAWNA WALTER
WITH HELEN CHISLETT

conran
OCTOPUS

To my babe of life whose undying faith in me
always challenges me to rise to the occasion and to
my mother, Gooch, who at 87 has such spirit and
energy that I can only hope to inherit.

First published in 1997 by
Conran Octopus Limited
37 Shelton Street
London WC2H 9HN

Commissioning Editor: Denny Hemming
Senior Editor: Jenna Jarman
Editorial Assistant: Helen Woodhall
Copy Editor: Catherine Ward

Designer: Karen Bowen
Picture Researcher: Rachel Davies
Production Controller: Suzanne Bayliss
Indexer: Hilary Bird

British Library Cataloguing-in-Publication Data
A catalogue record for this book is available
from the British Library

ISBN 1 85029 894 7

Printed and bound in China

CONTENTS

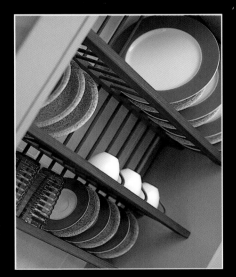

Organized living is about quality of life – the difference between constantly being surrounded by turmoil and being able to relax and enjoy your surroundings. It is a lifestyle path that I have always followed and which was the inspiration for both my company and my book.

Every day we are presented with different challenges and difficult decisions. As time goes on, our traditional approaches to both work and play are changing dramatically, and the home is taking on many additional roles – from workplace to the major source of entertainment and leisure activity.

Our home should be our sanctuary. A place where we feel totally at one with the world. We should surround ourselves with the things that have sentiment and meaning and which bring pleasure into our lives. We must learn to let go of things that we have collected along the way which no longer serve their function.

Throughout the book I have tried to offer some very simple solutions for taking the stress out of our daily routines. I have listened to the many people who visit The Holding Company who have given me words of organizational wisdom, and I now pass these on to you, along with our philosophy that organized living gives you more free time and that storage can be fun. I hope that with the help of this book you will enjoy getting and staying organized, and that this in turn will create more free time for the things that matter in life.

Dauna B. Walter

This minimalist hallway illustrates that storage
needn't be conventional or dull.
The poles, which are firmly secured to the wall,
are both witty and practical – intriguing when not
being used and, as long as they are never
overburdened, they also look stylish when providing
a home for coats and jackets.

GETTING

STARTED

YOU KNOW THERE MUST BE AN EASIER WAY TO LIVE YOUR LIFE THAN WHIRLING FROM ONE DOMESTIC CRISIS TO THE NEXT. YOU'RE SURE IT WOULD NEVER GET THIS BAD IF YOU LIVED IN A BIGGER HOUSE. AND YOU KNOW YOU WOULD BE ABLE TO GET SO MUCH MORE DONE IF YOU HAD JUST AN EXTRA HOUR IN THE DAY. AS FOR FINDING WHAT YOU NEED WHEN YOU NEED IT – WELL, YOU CAN BUT DREAM. SOUNDS FAMILIAR? YOU NEED TO SLOW DOWN, TAKE STOCK AND THINK AGAIN. HERE'S HOW TO CREATE SPACES YOU NEVER KNEW YOU HAD, FIND THOSE EXTRA HOURS AND BE ORGANIZED TO A TERRIFYING DEGREE.

S P A C E

There are two factors that affect the price of property more than all the others: how much space it offers; and where it is located. As the global population continues to swell, property prices continue to rise and compromises inevitably have to be made. So which one are you going to opt for: a roomy home in a second-rate location; or being squeezed on space, but living where you want?

It's a tough one. Architects and interior designers know that the future holds no easy answers: space will become an increasingly luxurious item, no matter which location you choose. One solution is to become ever more inventive about using space well.

Try looking on the bright side – small rooms are cheaper to heat than large ones; easier to clean; and you spend less money on possessions if you have nowhere to house them. Not that good design advice is directed only at those with limited space – in a larger home, you just have more room to make mistakes. Learn how to assess the space you have; how to prioritize what you need from it; and how to manipulate it to fit your needs. Good design is not an extra, it is the root of living well. Without it, you will never feel you are master or mistress of your own home.

Only by living in a space can you decide what is essential for your needs. It's not just about how much room you have – you must also consider the other people who live there: which areas are communal and which are private; what happens in these spaces; and what do people require from them?

The conventional ways of allotting functions to a room might not be the best for you. There's no commandment that says the living room must be on the ground floor and the bedrooms above; or that parents must have a larger bedroom than their children; or that partition walls must be left where they were first erected. This is your house – as long as you don't weaken it structurally, you can manipulate its spaces as you like.

The trick lies in assessing all the space – not just the obvious horizontal one, but the vertical too. Houses and apartments are full of 'dead space': high-level areas; nooks and crannies created by pipework and other architectural features; and basements and attics that are under-utilized. Design is about understanding and visualizing all the possibilities.

You might need the advice of a professional designer or architect, particularly if you're planning major structural alterations, but there's a lot you can do on your own with paper, pencil and a tape measure. Sketching a plan of your home, room by room, will help you focus on what you have, but you will only understand the options and limitations of the layout if you first live in the building. You need continually to make notes on aspects

Left Think in terms of spaces rather than rooms. You can manipulate your space according to your personal needs and create something much more dynamic and interesting into the bargain. Here, strong steel columns replace conventional partition walls, giving a bold, uncompromising feel.

Top Where barriers are needed, screens are an attractive alternative to walls. The sliding one in this converted loft space is a marker between hall and living space, and matches the style of the blinds.

Above Bamboo and rattan screens harmonize with the simplicity of this bedroom.

of it, such as traffic routes from room to room; light as it changes during the day; noise levels; and architectural features that you would like to keep (as well as those you would be happy to lose!).

Think about each room not only in terms of colours and styles, but also of what you expect from it and whether it serves its function well. In general terms, you have four options when it comes to improving a space.

Changing the function of a room

A guest room might become a home office, a dining room or a bedroom. This approach requires lateral thinking, but very little money. Be creative when assessing your spaces – if you have two adjoining bedroom closets, perhaps you can knock down the wall between them to create enough space for a bathroom? Then you can convert your bathroom into a small bedroom or study.

Changing the appearance of a room

Imagine the room emptied of furniture and furnishings; try to see how a different pattern or colour scheme or more sympathetic lighting could give it a whole new character. This is especially effective in small rooms where clever decoration can help hide their boxy appearance.

Changing the shape of a room

You can often improve awkwardly shaped rooms by slicing off extra space from an adjoining room – relocating partition walls can make this relatively easy. The removal of a fireplace can create a free wall for storage, and conventional doors can be replaced with sliding ones if space is really tight. You could even consider removing

the ceiling to create a cathedral-like vertical space with plenty of potential for a multi-layered look.

Changing by adding on

Conservatories have replaced lean-tos as the middle-class answer to adding a room, but there are other possibilities: a balcony can make all the difference to a bedroom; a porch where wet boots and dog leashes can be left will free up a hall and make it more inviting; or perhaps you can extend into unused basement or attic space? If

Opposite *Take a broad-minded approach when deciding on the functions of rooms and when arranging the furniture. This attic bedroom has a beautiful arched roof and the bed is positioned so that the sleeper can enjoy both the stars at night and the early-morning sunshine. The piano fits perfectly into the space created by the eaves.*

Below *The owner of this converted warehouse has made good use of vertical and horizontal space. A sturdy platform replaces the traditional upper storey, while the steps, which look as if they are suspended in thin air, leave the ground-floor view unimpeded.*

you have outbuildings with potential, look for ways of connecting these to the house.

By looking hard at the drawbacks of your home and the range of improvements that could be made, you should be able to narrow down what your real priorities are. Collect ideas from every source: tear out pages from magazines; consult neighbours and friends with similar houses; take advice and quotations from builders, architects, designers, plumbers, electricians, carpenters and anyone else who might have a role to play in helping you turn your ideas into reality. You might also need financial help, in which case all your drawings, notes and consultations will be useful in convincing a bank or other lender that you have really done your homework.

Planning

Once you are fired with enthusiasm for redesigning your space, the temptation will be to leap in straightaway. But don't be too hasty. You are still at idea level and need to explore the practicalities.

As with so many things in life, it all comes down to money, time and having to be realistic. Let's deal with money first. Apart from the headache of raising enough cash to carry out the proposed improvements, you also have to be reasonably certain that they will increase and not detract from the value of your home. This may not be so important to you if you own your house outright and have no plans to move. In any case, intelligent, thoughtful design has never yet caused property prices to fall through the floor.

Now to time – be honest about how competent and keen at these jobs you actually are. You want to love this house, not end up loathing it and resenting the loss of social life, hobbies and free weekends. Recognize which jobs you are able to take on yourself and which ones it is worth paying someone else to do. Remember that if you choose builders and other professionals carefully, they can often save you money by offering cheaper alternatives when your budget requires it.

As for being realistic, all kinds of modifications and improvements that look so easy on paper can turn into physical impossibilities when the structure of a house is examined. Networks of plumbing, wiring and heating components can make proposed changes far too expensive and risky to implement. You might also run foul of local planning laws.

All of this means that you must be flexible – and that means refining and re-examining your initial plan all the time.

Left *Pieces of furniture can also be utilized as screens. This display cabinet doubles as both valuable storage space and partition wall – a visual reminder to visitors that they are about to enter a work zone.*

Top *A bedroom closet has been converted into a compact bathroom – half-glazed doors prevent it from being claustrophobic.*

Above *The position of key pieces of furniture, movable screens and fixed cut-through partition walls combine to give this one-space apartment clearly identifiable zones.*

CULTURAL TRADITIONS

Good planning was a part of many ancient cultures and is not some mundane invention of twentieth-century thinking. When assessing your space, take a fresh look at some of these cultures for inspiration.

The ancient Chinese philosophy of feng shui is not just about using mirrors, plants, screens and bells to cure negative energy. It's also about the orientation of rooms and how, when and where to make changes to layout, furniture, decoration and lighting. Feng shui philosophers share the same basic principle as designers: deal with fundamentals first.

You can also draw inspiration from the rich culture of Japan. The traditional Japanese house embodies all the principles of simple, adaptable living spaces: main rooms open into each other, rather than onto corridors, so maximizing available space; partition walls are replaced by translucent paper screens that slide on wooden tracks and allow low-level dif-

Above *It's possible to take inspiration from other cultures and blend them with your own. This traditional Japanese-style interior exemplifies the purity and simplicity of oriental philosophy – from the gentle light filtering through the paper screens and the plain rush matting to the portable futon, and one object of beauty to meditate on: in this case, a simple white vase.*

Left *One wall of the room has been opened up to take some of the extra requirements of modern living – books, CDs and so on – yet the overall sense of calmness and order is not lost.*

fused light to filter through, bathing rooms in a soft glow. Wooden shutters at the windows keep out harsh weather and portable braziers provide heat for both warmth and cooking. Furniture is low level and kept to a minimum as kneeling is preferred to sitting, so the only essential items are futon beds and tatami mats stuffed with straw. Wall alcoves provide the perfect place to display pottery or paintings, but only one or two items at a time (which are changed regularly) to

focus attention on them. The art of restraint is practised in flower arranging, too, where one simple spray of flowers can be an object of intense beauty in uncluttered surroundings. How unlike many grand country houses, where every ornament seems to jostle for attention.

Another culture that has been revived and revered over the last few years is that of the Shakers, the religious community of Massachusetts that blossomed in the first half of the nineteenth century. Although

worlds apart from the Japanese, the Shakers had a surprising amount in common with them when furnishing their houses: a delight in natural materials, uncluttered surfaces and restrained colours. In fact, they were even more minimalist than the Japanese, as no decorative objects at all were tolerated. The more functional an object, the more perfect it was considered to be. It is this absence of decorative objects that makes Shaker interiors appear so orderly and spacious.

Shaker furniture is simple and elegant, with no veneers, inlays or decorative carving. Not that comfort was frowned upon: rocking chairs were commonplace in the kitchen. One of their most enduring contributions to design is the pegboard, which lined the walls of every room. The range of articles that could be hung here included the usual clothes, hats, towels and baskets and also the unexpected – clocks, chairs, tools and brooms. At the heart of their ethos was a conviction that everything should have its place in a home and that a house should be kept spotlessly clean. The former fed their ingenuity for creating storage places: chairs with lift-up seats where Bibles could be kept, and multi-armed hangers for clothes; their obsession with cleanliness resulted in castors on beds, drop-leaf tables, and chairs that could be pegged up out of the way when the floor was being swept. There's much that we can learn from the Shakers about the benefits of simple living.

Nomadic cultures also have much to teach us about focusing on essentials. There are few furnishings in the nomadic tents of the Sahara as everything has to be carried. Rugs and cushions replace chairs, and loose articles are carried in bags or boxes. The areas within the tent are not rigidly defined and there are no dominant pieces of furniture. In traditional Iraqi tents, cloths are hung up and used as screens when required.

It is in fact a modern characteristic to have strongly defined areas within the home and it's easy to forget that it has not always been like this. In the eighteenth century, there were no dining rooms in ordinary houses – you ate where you wanted to, simply pulling up a table and chair to do so. Purpose-built bathrooms are also a very new idea and, in fact, the tin bath in front of the fire was far more flexible. Nobody frowned if you entertained friends in your bedroom, held dances in your hallway or made love in your summer-house. Space constraints have become a strait-jacket on our thinking where our homes are concerned.

Above Shaker interiors are unmistakable for their shining cleanliness and absolute order. Furniture was admired for its simplicity, function and portability – no dust was allowed to gather underneath. Pegboards, the Shaker legacy we most admire today, were designed so that anything and everything could be lifted off a spotless floor. Often they were fixed at two heights, so that both adults and children could do their part in keeping the interior tidy.

Right Storage was another Shaker delight, but don't imagine that these drawers would have been a cluttered mess: everything had its rightful place.

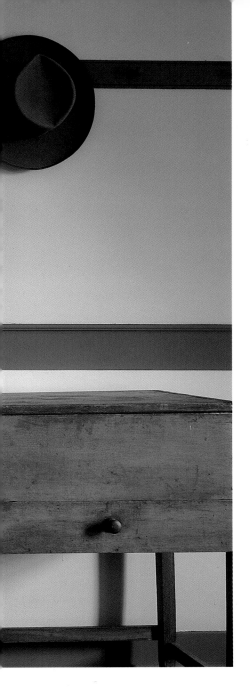

Left *Pegboards were not only used to store items such as brooms and hats — even the mirrors and towel rails were adapted to be hung from them. The jug and bowl were kept in a wooden tray to give a totally portable 'bathroom' that could be set down on any surface and the mirror is adjustable to suit all heights.*

Below *The Shakers were also very inventive when it came to designing dual-function furniture. The doors of this cabinet fold down to make two desk surfaces: an idea that manufacturers of modular furniture are still using today.*

SPACE-SAVING DESIGNS

Above In this cramped kitchen, the flip-down hot plates can be folded away after use so that the much-needed work surface is left free.
Below In a tiny apartment, an intimate dining room is transformed quickly and easily into a luxurious sleeping area when the furniture is carried out of sight and the doors of the armoire opened up to reveal the fold-down bed.
Opposite If space is at a premium in your house, why not draw inspiration from a traditional Romany caravan, where lack of space does not necessarily mean fewer possessions – just a carefully formulated system for storing and displaying them.

There are two approaches you can take when rethinking the space you have. The first is to follow the example of Eastern and nomadic cultures and blur the boundaries between the rooms: open up spaces by knocking down partition walls; create new ones by converting an understairs cupboard; or employ redundant ones such as an attic or basement. The second is to explore the ergonomics of space-saving designs: caravans (trailers), canal boats and space shuttles are examples of this genre.

Storage space is everywhere: hidden behind panels in ceilings and walls; tucked under mattresses; squeezed behind pipes; or concealed in beds. Bottom-hinged cupboard doors flip down to become tables; beds drop down from walls; and fridges, televisions and radios are housed in custom-made cabinets. These inventive solutions arise out of the constraints of the surroundings and prove the point that design problems can stimulate really creative and exciting approaches.

If you are designing around a very tight space – a studio apartment or converted warehouse, for example – why not visit a caravan (trailer) or boat show and pick up some ideas on how to make the most efficient use of that space?

Don't imagine that capsular living has to mean dull and characterless surroundings – visit a Romany caravan and you will be impressed by the beautiful plates and pots, as well as unexpected details such as stone fireplaces and rocking chairs. Yet everything has its place.

A foot in both camps probably makes most sense. You need to find out how to make the most of the space you have, so that you never feel cramped and visitors are barely aware of how little there really is, and you need to explore storage solutions to hide away all the clutter that's part of real life. Don't treat function as the poor relation to decoration. Perhaps your dream home is a stately country residence with a myriad servants to do your bidding, but don't forget that the grandeur and opulence of life above stairs needs efficient, simple work rooms below.

SYSTEM S

Being organized isn't just about finding things quickly or getting more done. It's about improving the quality of your life. If you've ever bemoaned the fact that you never have time these days for painting, yoga or sunning yourself in the garden, then you have not learned to organize your time efficiently. If you can adopt new systems of running the house that save you five minutes here and ten minutes there, and use all that saved time to do the things you always wanted to do, then you will be a happier person. Life doesn't have to be a continuous battle to maintain a house and all the possessions in it – slim down those possessions, simplify the house, make sure everything can be put away quickly and easily, and you will discover that life needn't be such an uphill slog. This isn't about being unable to enjoy just lounging around for an hour or two, but it is about freeing up your time and energy to do the things that are fun and satisfying without feeling guilty about the state of your kitchen. A chaotic house results only in muddled thinking and wasted energy. Call it good karma, good feng shui or just plain common sense – the message is the same: if your house is clean, uncluttered and calming, you will find your state of mind to be the same.

EVALUATING WHAT YOU HAVE

Everyone should ask themselves this question and answer it honestly: am I master of all my possessions, or do they dominate me? It is a stark fact that most of us own too many things, that we accumulate more as we get older, and that our houses become choked with redundant and rejected items. Do you even know what you do own? For most of us, clearing out a closet takes hours because we find whole piles of things that we had simply forgotten we had.

All this clutter and waste is a direct result of the consumer society in which we live. Not for us the simplicity of a rolled bed, a bowl to eat from and a blanket to keep out the cold. We have literally thousands of possessions, but how many do we actually value or need?

The time has come for a radical rethink. Choose a room in the house and look at what is there. Which items are you hanging on to out of habit? Which ones can be thrown away now? Which ones are

worth keeping, but have no place of their own to be kept in? How do the things in this room make you feel? Comfortable? Depressed? Happy? Does someone else need these things more than you do?

Don't leap in and try to sort out years of hoarding in half a day. Set yourself one task and a rough time limit: maybe it's a half-hour job or maybe it will take half a day. Perhaps there's a cupboard full of junk that you always meant to sort out and never have, which might take a couple of

Ask yourself why you're hoarding them. With most people, it's not so much insecurity as laziness: if you keep hiding things away you never have to make a decision about keeping them. The truth is that if you've managed not to use them for this long and owning them is not going to improve the overall quality of your life, then you should let them go. Perhaps there's a way of recycling them for a good cause? Maybe you could take them to a charity shop, sell them or give them to

Left *The most ordered of homes are those with limited personal effects. The first step to organizing your home – and ultimately your life – is to pare down your belongings so that you only need to find space for those that you love and need. Everything else is a waste of space.*

Below *Like the bedroom opposite, this living space is elegant, tranquil and calming not so much because of what is in it, but because of what is not. Natural wood, white linens and squeaky clean surfaces combine to give a feeling of structure and order in the owner's life.*

hours. But sorting through piles of old magazines or paperback books might only take an hour. Reward yourself after completing each chore: run a hot bath or pour yourself a glass of chilled wine.

Each task should result in three piles: things you want to get rid of; things you want to hold on to, but store away; and things you want to keep on view or close at hand. Take a look at that first pile – those unwanted gifts, sad shopping mistakes and never-to-be repaired gadgets.

someone whose need really is greater than your own. Recycling is important psychologically because it makes you feel good – not just about having cleared things out, but also about having benefited someone else.

Once you start on this path, you might find yourself moving some things from the second pile to the first. The second pile should include things of sentimental value; out-of-season possessions, such as Christmas tree decorations or winter coats; or items you are storing for your children until they have a home of their own. They need to be wrapped and boxed, then labelled clearly and stored somewhere out of sight – in the attic, in the basement or on top of a cupboard.

Now to the final pile. Do these things have a recognizable home of their own where they can be put away when you have finished using them? If not, can you make one? Do you need to build or buy something ready-made, be it a hook or a cabinet? Are there other similar items that can be stored together? The secret of

efficient storage is to keep like with like. Drawers or cupboards filled with miscellanea are often the slippery slope to creating a corner of chaos.

Just ponder for a moment the efficiency of a cutlery drawer. There's a place for knives, for forks, for different-sized spoons and so on. In your home you need to create a similar system where everything has a home. Before you buy major items or decorative pieces, think about where they're going to go. Will you throw something away to make room for them? Are they going to add to the quality of your life? Are they beautiful or functional?

Remember that writing that cheque isn't the end of the story. Everything you buy is an investment, and you have a responsibility to maintain your possessions well by treating them with respect, repairing them when necessary, storing them efficiently and cleaning them regularly. This all takes time. If your dried flowers are gathering dust, or your shoes need re-heeling yet again, you should question whether they are worth keeping.

Once you've scaled down what you own into a more manageable amount, you have to tackle the way in which you and your family use the home. Find systems and routines that work for all of you. For example, if clean laundry is always left around for a few days in piles before being put away, resolve to tackle it more quickly. It only takes five or ten minutes to fold up clothes and sort them into drawers, so do it at once. It only takes a minute to put yesterday's newspapers in the recycling bin, so do it straightaway. The same applies to unloading the dishwasher, putting shoes out of sight or cleaning the dog's bowl. Don't let these tiny little jobs build up into one huge task that's going to take an hour or so of your time when you do get around to it, and which will prey on your mind in the meantime. Tasks that hang over from day to day are stressful.

Enlist the help of those who live with you. Discuss which chores have to be done daily, weekly, monthly. Decide together how they should be tackled. The reward will be of its own making –

everyone feels good in a clean, comfortable environment. Children might need coaxing, but they could earn a little extra spending money for taking on certain responsibilities or be rewarded with extra time to do the things they want. Show them that organized living doesn't mean not having fun, but means creating more time to do the things that are fun, such as going on a bike ride, taking a trip to the swimming pool or seeing a film. If children can see the personal benefits of tidying up quickly, then they will be happy to do so.

It's important that no one person is left to take on all the stress and responsibility of implementing a new, organized way of life. It might be that rotas will help, or drawing up a few ground rules (such as always cleaning the bath after use), or agreeing which parts of the house can be messy and which stay tidy. But retain some flexibility at this stage – there's no point in being so regimental that no-one feels comfortable in their own home. Of course there will be days when you fling all the junk behind the sofa or under the bed. But the difference is knowing that you will set time aside later to sort it out before it gets out of hand. It's about recognizing that a little bit of self-discipline goes a long, long way.

Life would be very boring if everyone's home looked the same, and the principles of organized living aren't restricted to minimalist interiors. Rather it's about deciding the priorities in your own home: what you do there, who shares it with you, what makes you feel good. You can have as many possessions as you want –

hundreds of videos or stacks of glossy magazines – but try to store them in such a way that you can use them and enjoy them whenever you want.

Once you are in total control of your environment, you can plan other activities much more easily. The difference between people who paint, write books or learn languages and those who only talk about doing these things is good time management. Once you've created extra pockets of time, it's up to you how you use them.

Left This room exudes confidence – from the vertical, column-style radiator to the boat-like daybed. The free-standing storage unit in front of the window contains all the extras of life – books, magazines and directories – so that they don't encroach on the surrounding area.

***Below** Storage furniture is as important to a house as a bed, table or chair. This cabinet with roll-down blinds is perfect for hiding plain cardboard files.*

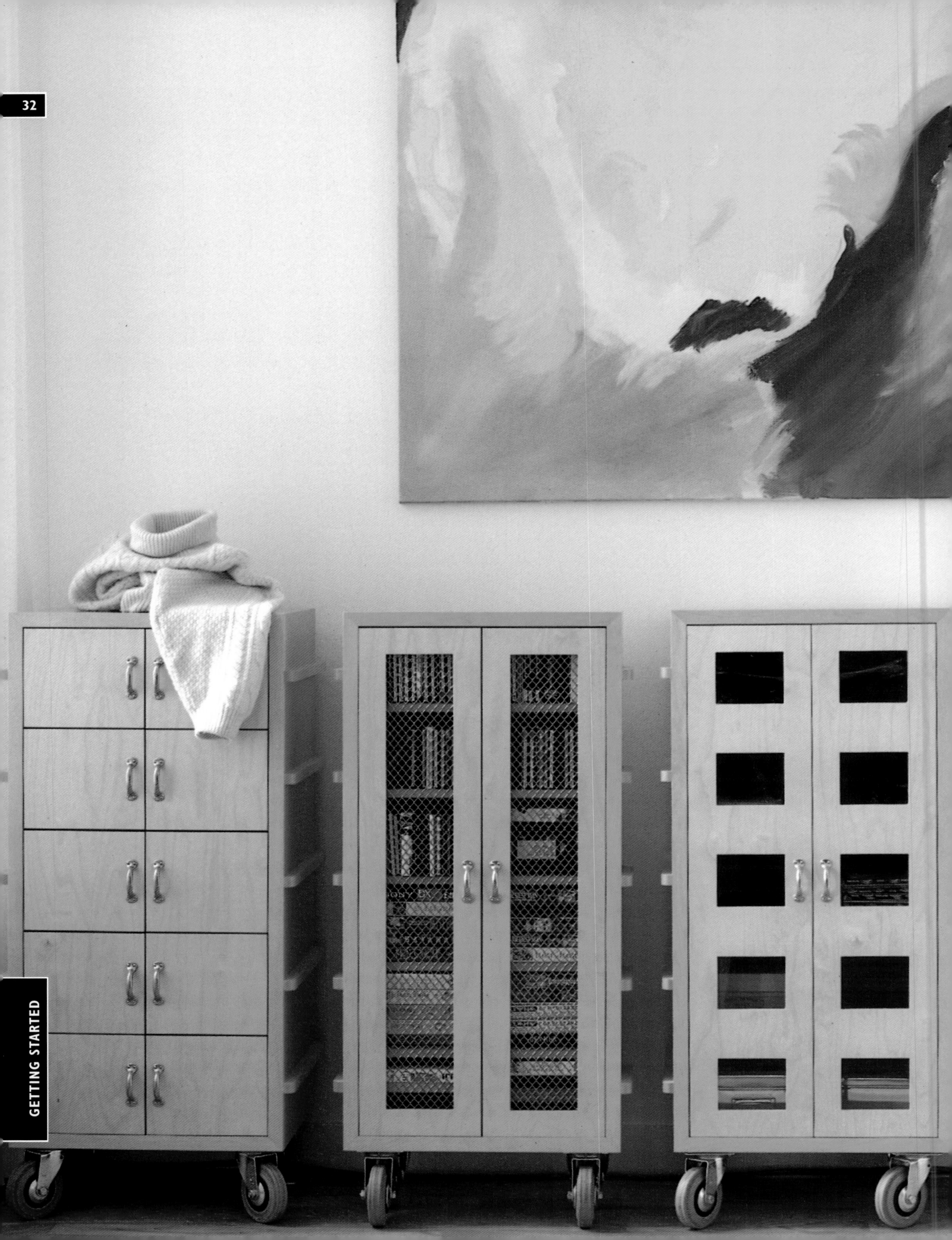

STORAGE

For too long now storage has been the poor relation of design. Flick back through old glossy home-interest titles and what you notice is how pure, how perfect, how unblemished most of the interiors are. Where are the books, the videos, the children's toys, the newspapers or the muddy boots? It isn't just that they're out of sight – there's no acknowledgement of their existence at all. The down-to-earth approach of today has taken a more honest line and one that's necessary when space is at a premium. Designers are facing up to all the household clutter and looking for ways of storing or displaying it effectively – in fact, more often than not, they're making it an integral part of the house's style. The message is clear: don't be ashamed of what you own; don't try to pretend that unsightly essentials don't exist or that real life can be equated with magazine pages. Instead, learn to deal with it.

Storage is about choices: free-standing or built-in; old or new; large or small; ready-made or made-to-measure. At the end of the day, it's all about having something to contain other things and the options are as numerous and as covetable as your possessions. So look at it afresh and embrace it with a passion.

STORAGE OPTIONS

Now that you recognize the need for more storage in the home, you are faced with decisions about what needs storing and where. You will have to consider whether to go for a built-in storage system or a free-standing product; whether to improvise with what you already own by making some structural or aesthetic alterations; or whether to box up all the excess and store it away long-term. Perhaps you have some items you want to display and others you want to hide? Or maybe you need solutions in keeping with the style of your house?

You need to analyse what you own and how accessible it needs to be. You have to assess the storage you already have, how effective it is, and the ideal way to improve it. Budget is a consideration too, so you will also have to apply imaginative thinking to some storage problems.

Don't just dwell on the big items, such as toy cupboards or kitchen clutter. Make a note of the small things that irritate you because you can never find them: the television remote control, for example, or your children's dental appointment cards. Resolve to come up with a system that works: make a space somewhere, buy a suitable container, and determine to put things back each time you use them.

Obviously you can't solve all your home's storage problems in one fell swoop, but you can highlight the least efficient areas of the house – the home office, maybe, or the bedroom closet – and resolve to make an impact here before taking on anything else. If you enjoy problem solving or puzzles, then think of

tackling storage dilemmas in this light: what you need more of; where it should be sited; how it will fit into the room; and whether it is affordable.

You also have to consider long-term storage for out-of-season or seldom used items: here storage isn't just about tidiness, but also about protecting your things. Do you need to invest in special bags or hangers, for example? Even on a day-to-day basis, the right storage can add considerably to the life of your possessions.

Left A wall of storage is a valuable asset in any home. These built-in cupboards extend over the door frame, which has been deepened accordingly. Frosted glass doors allow a tempting glimpse of what's inside, without giving too much away.
Above Storage is obviously an important consideration in this kitchen because it extends from floor to ceiling, making maximum use of the available space. It combines both displayed and concealed areas – the latter hidden within baskets rather than behind doors. Open shelves are not only practical but also create an interesting focal point.

Decorative collections need to be thought about too – a badly displayed one might look a mess, but given a little more thought it can become an interesting focal point. Architectural features, such as niches and shelves, help you to create display areas for treasured collections or items of visual interest. You can choose to put these up high´ or at eye level. By painting the background or framing them in some way, you can give them more impact.

As you walk from room to room, try to spot the chaos zones and come up with a suitable solution – it might be that your clothes, your video tapes or your files are a mess. Tackle each area with gusto – mail order catalogues, kitchen and bathroom shops, and other specialized stores are a great source of ideas as well as products. The result – clutter-free spaces and hassle-free living – will, with luck, impress other members of the household who will soon be demanding more shelf space, clothes rails or attractive containers. Like all good habits, once you get the bug, you won't know how you ever coped before.

Open shelves or built-in cupboards are easy ways to increase available storage. You might decide to lose a small amount of space from a room and create a whole wall of storage, or it might be that you requisition wasted space, such as under the eaves or in an alcove, for better use. Perhaps this is a simple enough job for you to do yourself, or you know a good joiner who can create exactly the effect you want. Either way, make sure the design you

The disadvantage of built-in furniture is that you can't take it with you if you move, but the other side of the coin is that buyers might look more favourably on your home when you come to sell. It's impossible to say whether built-in furniture will be more or less expensive than free-standing – each type comes in ranges at both the top and the bottom end of the market. The most important thing is that you explore all the possibilities before coming to a final decision.

are planning will integrate well into the room and that it can be painted or finished in sympathy with existing styles and materials in the house.

Remember that built-in furniture has another advantage over its free-standing counterparts – the shelves or cupboards can be customized exactly to take the objects you want them to. This means that you will be able to fit much more into this space than if you had simply bought something ready-made.

Far left *This fold-down table and stools that can be easily brought out when necessary are perfect for a tiny space.*
Left *In a modern dining room, flat doors take on the appearance of stacked cubes; clutter is hidden and a disciplined image is maintained.*
Above left *The walls of storage in this passageway have been muted to blend in with the surroundings. Only the door handles give a clue as to what's actually here.*
Above right *A feature is made of rolled towels on cubed shelving in this sloping bathroom.*

If you intend to buy something for a specific purpose, then go cautiously. It's all too easy to be seduced by the style and look of a piece of furniture, when deep down you know it's too small or too deep or the wrong colour for the location you have in mind. Size isn't everything: you might see an antique linen press cupboard that will create huge amounts of storage space, but if the interior isn't right for your needs it will be a waste of space rather than an efficient use of it. Don't settle for second best, and keep looking around – there are so many purpose-built pieces of storage furniture on the market that it must be possible to find one that fulfils perfectly both its functional and aesthetic purposes.

You have two options when it comes to buying free-standing furniture: you can choose a piece that serves some storage need – such as a wardrobe, bookcase, armoire, chest-of-drawers or home leisure cabinet – or you can buy a modular set that doesn't stand as a piece of furniture in its own right, but is sold in kit form and can be extended or amended as your needs change. These are available in many different styles which can either be left plain or painted, varnished or stencilled to fit in with your surroundings. Your decision will be based on the style of your home, your budget, your personal taste and what you require from the furniture. A modular system can be practical in a child's bedroom or home office, but you may not be so happy installing it in the living room, where it could begin to look dated very quickly.

Above *Glazed doors leave you no other option but to display the contents. This creates a focal point, but be warned: anything on display must be rigorously cleaned and presented at its most attractive.*
Right *The Victorian green of this toy cupboard is a perfect backdrop to the nostalgic collection of toys.*
Top right *If you prefer to conceal your wares in drawers, then you might like to choose something with strong visual interest like these rows of studs.*
Far right *Clever brushwork and a confident approach can transform the ugliest piece of furniture into something really covetable.*

Many industrial storage ideas are now becoming acceptable in domestic situations – utility carts, lockers and racks can all look quite at home in the right setting, and they offer strong, portable and generous storage. Many are even fitted with castors, making them easy to move from one room to the next. If your taste is more antique than hi-tech, there are plenty of coffers, chests, cupboards and dressers to choose from. Pay attention to the interior as well as the exterior when buying any piece of storage furniture. Ideally it should be organized so that everything contained within it has its own place. There's no point investing in something to take all the junk if it is so poorly organized that it tumbles out on the floor every time you open the door.

Don't forget that there are plenty of products on the market to help you customize the interior of an existing piece of furniture should you need to. Under-shelf baskets, multi-armed hangers and nests of storage boxes are just a few of the solutions you might consider.

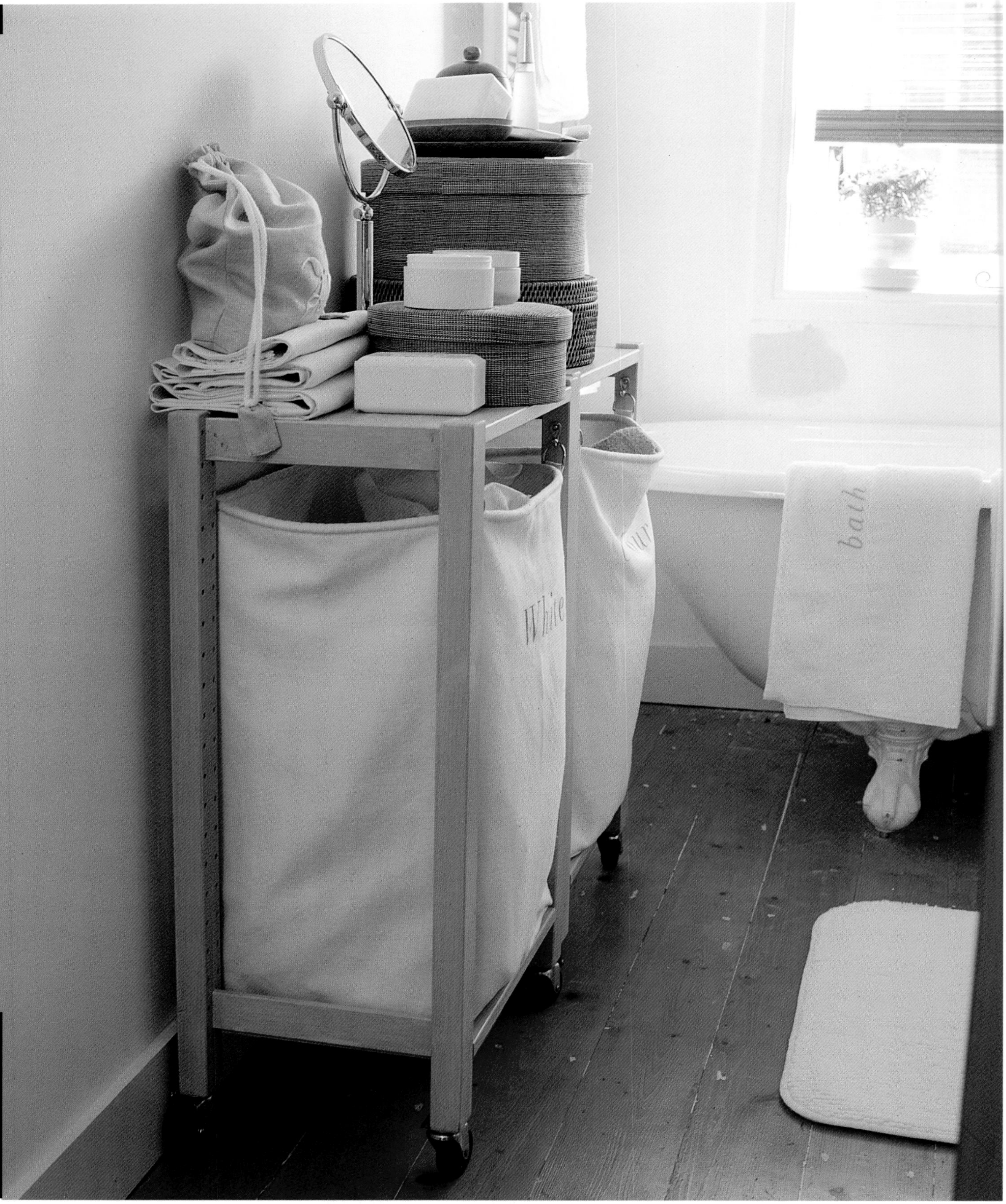
White
bath

Left and Opposite When organizing your storage, you need to find a home for everything you own – no matter how small and inconsequential. This trolley (cart) is an excellent design, combining large canvas bags for dirty linen with surfaces for stacking boxes of different sizes.

Below The open shelves of a bedside cabinet have been given a new dimension with the addition of bought-to-measure baskets – an attractive way of concealing some of your personal possessions.

Right Wire trays are a practical alternative in the bathroom where conditions are hot and steamy.

Flick through the pages of a mail order catalogue selling storage items or visit your local department store and you'll be amazed by the variety, ingenuity and beauty of the containers on offer. If you want to put your home in order, then you couldn't pick a better time to do it.

Rediscover those things that have always been around, but which you have never valued until now: the humble box, the simple basket, the excellent jar. Look around your home and you will find all sorts of containers that you could put to good use – perhaps you have something that's ideal for rubber bands, pencils, postage stamps, paperclips, picture hooks or screws? What about safety pins, cotton balls, or dental picks? Why keep everything in a muddle when it's so easy to separate things and store like with like in jam jars, empty chocolate boxes, old mustard pots or shoe boxes? Bear in mind that the right containers can revolutionize a piece of furniture by filling up every bit of space to make it much more efficient.

One of the most appealing things about containers is their versatility. Not only can you find one that suits exactly the scale and shape of the item you want to store, but you can also find one to suit the style of your own home. Rather than go for a muddled motley selection, why not try to keep them all co-ordinating from room to room: plain white or matt black plastic; pretty wicker or grey card; silver metal or clear glass?

Baskets are an absolute must in most homes – they can be used for storing everything from newspapers and toys to letters or oranges. They come in every conceivable shape and size: tall for umbrellas, sturdy for logs, small for the dressing table, lightweight for laundry. Boxes are another must: you can choose from patterned paper or coloured plastic, plain wood or chic cardboard – whatever suits your home. You can even make dividers to organize the space inside the boxes. If you invest in containers that give you pleasure, putting things away will never seem a chore again.

As well as traditional containers, there are custom-made items to suit every need and eventuality. If your drawers are a mess, then there are dividers to separate socks from underpants or bras from tights. Not only that, but you can then use sock dividers to keep them in pairs, or create more drawer space by hanging ties and belts on customized hangers.

There are organizers for everything from earrings and children's hair bows to shoe brushes and loose change. There's nothing to stop you making your own versions once you get the general idea — you need only the basic cutting, sticking and sewing skills to make your own and you could ask the kids to join in.

Of course, storage is not just about containers. Remember to use wall space to the full: the under-rated hook has a lot of potential for hats, hangers, framed collections or wall-hung organizers. Put up pinboards for letters, bills, shopping lists and other reminders; and frame collections of your children's drawings or poems and hang them on the wall.

Finally, keep reassessing your storage needs. Every six months or so, take another look around and ask yourself whether systems are still working as well as you wanted them to, and whether you need to set up new ones to cover different areas. Can some more space be utilized or another load of redundant stuff be cleared out? We are not static creatures — our homes change and develop as we do. But once you have embraced the basic principles of organized living, you will find it easy to continue using them.

Top left If you enjoy cooking, you probably like to work with everything you use on display. Why hide essential utensils in a drawer and waste time rummaging around for them when you could store the most frequently used items in a pot like this one?
Above Be imaginative about storage — test tubes on a stand make the perfect home for dried herbs and spices and look attractive too.
Right If you don't have a chest-of-drawers, boxes will do. Here, a tower of chic metal ones makes an effective filing system for socks, lingerie and folded clothes — who says they should be limited to paper?

ROOM BY ROOM

NOW YOU'VE HAD A GLIMPSE OF HOW YOU COULD LIVE, IT'S TIME TO START THE SERIOUS WORK. **W**HICH ROOM STRESSES YOU OUT EVERY TIME YOU WALK PAST IT, NEVER MIND INTO IT? **W**ELL, THAT'S WHERE YOU SHOULD BEGIN. **T**URN TO THE RELEVANT SECTION AND FIND OUT HOW BEST TO ASSESS WHAT YOU ALREADY HAVE; PRIORITIZE WHAT YOU MOST NEED; FOCUS ON THE PROBLEMS; AND FIND THE SOLUTIONS. **R**EMEMBER THE GOLDEN RULE: DIVIDE AND CONTAIN. **T**HAT IS THE KEY TO KNOCKING ORDER INTO ANY SPACE, FROM THE LARGEST LIVING ROOM TO THE SMALLEST BATHROOM CABINET.

ONE-ROOM LIVING

The idea of living in one room may conjure up images of a small, cramped bed-sit with a one-ring stove, but as you will see from the following pages the reality is often far removed from that depressing image. Indeed, more and more people would rather live in a studio-style apartment in an upmarket area, albeit with limited space, than in a down-market one. To cope with demand, warehouses, factories and other industrial buildings are being divided into apartments, providing new awareness of what one-room living can offer: acres of space and endless opportunities. One thing is certain: living in one room need not mean cramping your style, but it does mean having a disciplined approach. Not only must you reconsider all your possessions in the light of what it is practical and worthwhile to keep – no more impulse buying – but you have to face the ugly truth that all your possessions will be permanently on display for every visitor to see. That is, unless you can think of some ingenious ways to conceal the unsightly and embarrassing. Then you'll need some inspired ideas about storing everything else. Not everyone has the confidence to live in this manner, but for those who do – all the room's a stage.

ASSESSING SPACE

One-room living might be a challenge, but it can be a satisfying one if you rise to it. Indeed, many designers would argue that planning a one-room apartment often yields excellent results because the self-discipline required means that only objects that really count make the grade.

Consider the following guidelines when assessing your space and be ruthless when it comes to organizing your belongings. In houses where space is at a premium, every single object should either have a recognizable function, or give you such pleasure as an object that you cannot bear to be without it. Lightweight or portable objects are useful because they offer flexibility, as do those that serve more than one function or that can be hidden away after use – not just sofas that convert into beds but tables that collapse, trolleys (carts) that double as tables and baskets that stack.

You might only have one room, but with artful thinking you can divide up the space and create distinctive areas. Write down all the functions you and your co-habitees require from this space. To avoid driving each other mad, you must find ways of introducing some private corners into your shared territory. If structural changes aren't an option, you could do this with screens or furniture to create partitions for anything from working, cooking and bathing to sleeping, entertaining or watching television.

Colour is another good way of defining areas of a room – you might use a subtle colour change for each one, anchoring them together with a bright rug or striking upholstery fabric. Base your choice of colours on which time of day you are most often there – light, airy shades for daytime; strong, dark ones for night-time. Don't make the mistake of thinking that only white will brighten up a dingy room – try yellow instead, with a shot of lime green, or neutrals with a flash of citrus. It's best to avoid pattern on the walls of small rooms unless you're a skilled decorator, but introduce it in other features of the room like rugs, furnishing fabrics, cushions or lamps.

Lighting can alter the mood of a room dramatically, so make sure yours is as flexible as possible because reading, entertaining, working and dressing all need quite different strengths and directions of light. Don't limit yourself to a central pendant – place various types of matching lamps around the room to create more intimate areas for reading and relaxing.

If you have the money, there are some ingenious products on the market to help make the most of limited space: swing-out bookcases, portable storage cubes, hidden closets. In fact, the irony of one-room living is that it can cost a great deal to design and furnish well. But it needn't be like that – if you plan your room with imagination and treat your furniture with flexibility, you should be able to create an exciting and individual effect.

Left *When you live in one space, everything you own is on display both to yourself and to visitors. You might not be able to conceal the bed, but you can make sure it's always neatly made up, clean and uncluttered by personal mess. This studio presents a perfect front – everything is carefully placed, well chosen and maintained to the highest degree.*
Above left *This apartment is more relaxed in tone, but all those open shelves do, in fact, demand a lot of maintenance.*
Above *The clever use of one strong colour – here, cobalt blue – can unify the different zones of a one-room apartment and make it appear larger than it actually is.*

Above *Solidly constructed raised platforms often replace the traditional second storey in one-space apartments. The sleeping area here is in fact tiny, but it benefits not just from the feeling of space below but also from the French doors leading out onto an attractive balcony.*

Right *This raised bed has a very cozy feel, the books, flowers and pictures all combining to make a bold statement about the owner's priorities in life. Pyramid-style edging makes an interesting barrier and encourages the sleeper to feel more secure in his or her roost.*

One-space homes can too easily turn into enormous bedrooms. The bed itself is a dominant feature because it takes up so much room and while a sofa bed gives you instant dual-function living, it's tedious to make up and strip on a daily basis. If you prefer a proper bed, make sure it offers as much storage as possible – under-bed drawers are the ideal place for bulky things like sports equipment or out-of-season clothes. Make sure there are surfaces around the bed for essentials like books, reading glasses or a phone, but don't allow them to become cluttered with personal effects – everything from cufflinks and nail polish to contact lenses and lipstick must have a recognized home.

Unless you don't mind having everything you own on permanent display, one of the first things you must tackle is how to store such items. Built-in closets are the obvious solution, but at the other end of the financial scale you might opt for a clothes rail on wheels. Bear in mind that one-room living doesn't only mean being disciplined about where things are kept, it's also about having systems and dealing with things immediately: clean laundry must be folded up and put away at once, make-up must be put back in drawers and shoes must be tidied away. To help you with this, learn how to organize your wardrobe efficiently – separate long-hanging clothes from short-hanging ones to create extra storage space underneath the short garments. You can either add another rail below these, so doubling your hanging space, or buy a set of

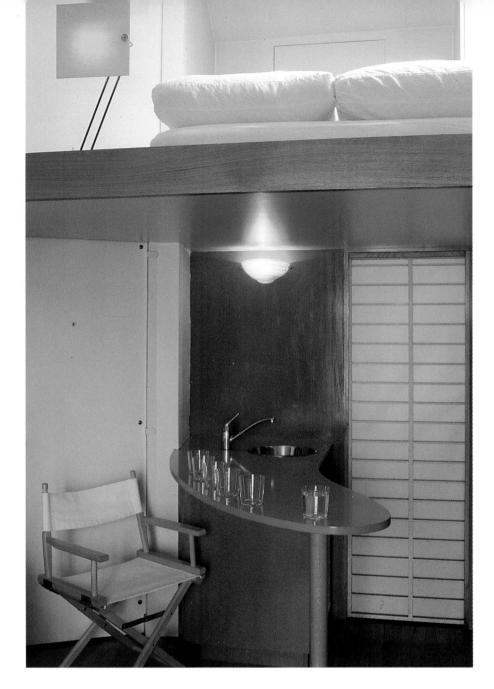

stackable cubes for folded clothes or shoes. Out-of-season clothes must be stored properly, so pack them into boxes and put them on high-level shelves or cupboard tops. If you go right through a season without wearing a certain outfit, the time has come to throw it away. The same applies to clothes that you never get around to repairing or shoes that are too worn to mend. When space is precious, you have no alternative but to be absolutely ruthless with your possessions.

Above This sophisticated high-level sleeping area replaces the conventional ceiling that would normally separate two storeys. The owner's needs are catered for with a light set into the platform and a sink plumbed into the kidney-shaped work-surface below. It takes the eye of a professional to see these sorts of possibilities, but if you're working with a very cramped space and have a budget that would allow for custom-built solutions, you might consider hiring an architect or designer to come up with ideas which, in the long term, could reap huge rewards.

Cooking and bathing areas need careful planning if they are going to be integrated into the space as a whole. If you want to create a coherent look, it is important that each zone should merge imperceptibly with the next.

In terms of appliances, a kitchen can be as compact as you want. Obviously you will need something to cook food on or with, but this needn't mean a conventional stove. A microwave oven offers a neat and practical solution, but you might also have room for a two-ring hob (cooktop) – this can be built into your work surface if you're really short on space. Choose the largest sink that is practical in the given space and make sure there's a work surface or drainage area nearby. A place for storing food is the third essential and this will mean a fridge and cupboard space. Again, choose an appliance that suits your needs – if you eat a lot of frozen meals, a fridge-freezer might be a good investment.

In terms of storage, you will need somewhere for cooking pans and utensils, cleaning supplies, food, crockery and cutlery. Use vertical space as well as horizontal – ceiling racks with hooks for pots and pans take up little space. Look for ways of utilizing cupboards to the full – fixed shelves tend to waste space (unless they're customized to suit your needs), but you can add wire racks and under-shelf trays to maximize the available room. One final point in the kitchen: don't cram cupboards with useless gadgets – a food processor with choice of blades can fulfil most functions.

The bathroom is where you keep many of your most personal belongings and for this reason you will need an effective storage system to hide away all your things when not in use. Work out which ones are attractive enough to have on permanent display and place these on open shelves. The rest can be stored out of sight. There are plenty of bathroom cabinets on the market – not just conventional wall-hung medicine cabinets, but also more attractive free-standing units for

storing towels and linen. If you can't afford to splash out on new bathroom furniture, look for ingenious places that you can exploit for extra storage, such as panels or platforms around the bath, under-basin hideaways or narrow nooks and crannies created by pipework. To make life easier, classify your belongings according to type: first aid, nail care, hair products, shaving gear and so on. There are plenty of attractive containers on the market to help keep your bathroom in order.

Above Introducing too many partitions into your space can make it feel cramped and claustrophobic. Sometimes it's better to put everything you have bravely on display – not just in the kitchen, but in the bathroom area too.

Top right Here, the bath is tucked into a corner near to the sofa, and identical window treatments and cool colours pull the whole area together.

Right A barn-like space reveals an interesting use of partitions – some solid, like the panelled divider, and some only suggestive, such as the rattan blind hung above the television.

LEISURE AND WORK

The general all-purpose living area will probably be defined by a layout of comfortable seating, tables and home leisure equipment: television, CD player, computer and so on. Many activities go on here, from talking to friends and reading books to practising yoga. As well as assessing what you most often use this area for, you must also consider what items need to be near at hand and how best to conceal or display them. Living rooms are never static, so try to design a layout that can be altered easily depending on what is going on there at the time. Most importantly, there should be plenty of surfaces handy to house all the items that find their way into this area – from books, magazines and newspapers to videos, mail and CDs.

Maybe you're going to be sharing this space with children or teenagers. It might not be the ideal basis for family life, but you can make it work. The secret is to define certain areas as child zones and provide enough storage there to scoop toys and games out of sight when not in use. In this type of situation, it's important that everyone learns to follow some basic rules: no excess junk; tidying up once something is finished with; and storing like with like. If something offends your eyes so much you can barely stand to see it, then there's only one solution and that is to hide it. Buy folding screens that can be positioned to hide little corners of chaos.

A home office is another area that has the potential to make one-room living sheer misery. But you can make it work if you vow not to become a slave to paper. You need a desk or similar surface; your computer, phone and fax; and enough shelves and drawers to store stationery, files and accounts. If you invest in a filing cabinet, choose one that will merge imperceptibly into the rest of the room or else customize one that doesn't. If you make a dedicated effort to erase excess paper from your life, you will find it possible to store what you need in very little space, so deal with mail immediately – respond to it, file it or bin it – and regularly cull all out-of-date material.

Top and above *If space is at a premium, it might be worth investing in some dual-purpose furniture. Designs like this are ingenious for concealing your office equipment when a dining table is required.*
Opposite *In this sophisticated apartment, the work space is contained and well planned – white surfaces and natural materials suggest that it has been designed for daytime use. By contrast, the darkness of the dining furniture and tableware signal night-time intimacy. The two zones are not at odds with each other, but send out contrasting signals that remove the need for physical divisions.*

TIPS

- High-level storage is crucial. Invest in a good-looking ladder that enables you to gain access without difficulty.
- For low-level storage, look at units which fit under the bed and can be wheeled out when needed.
- Keep colour schemes simple and light to make space appear larger.
- Movable furniture is essential – castors with locking brakes are a must.
- Use fabric screens to cover ugly areas – they look wonderful and protect your things from dust.
- Choose multi-purpose work surfaces.
- To utilize wall space, consider tables, beds and desks that can be fixed vertically to the wall.
- Choose dual-purpose furniture – chairs with lift-up lids or washing machines that double as dryers.

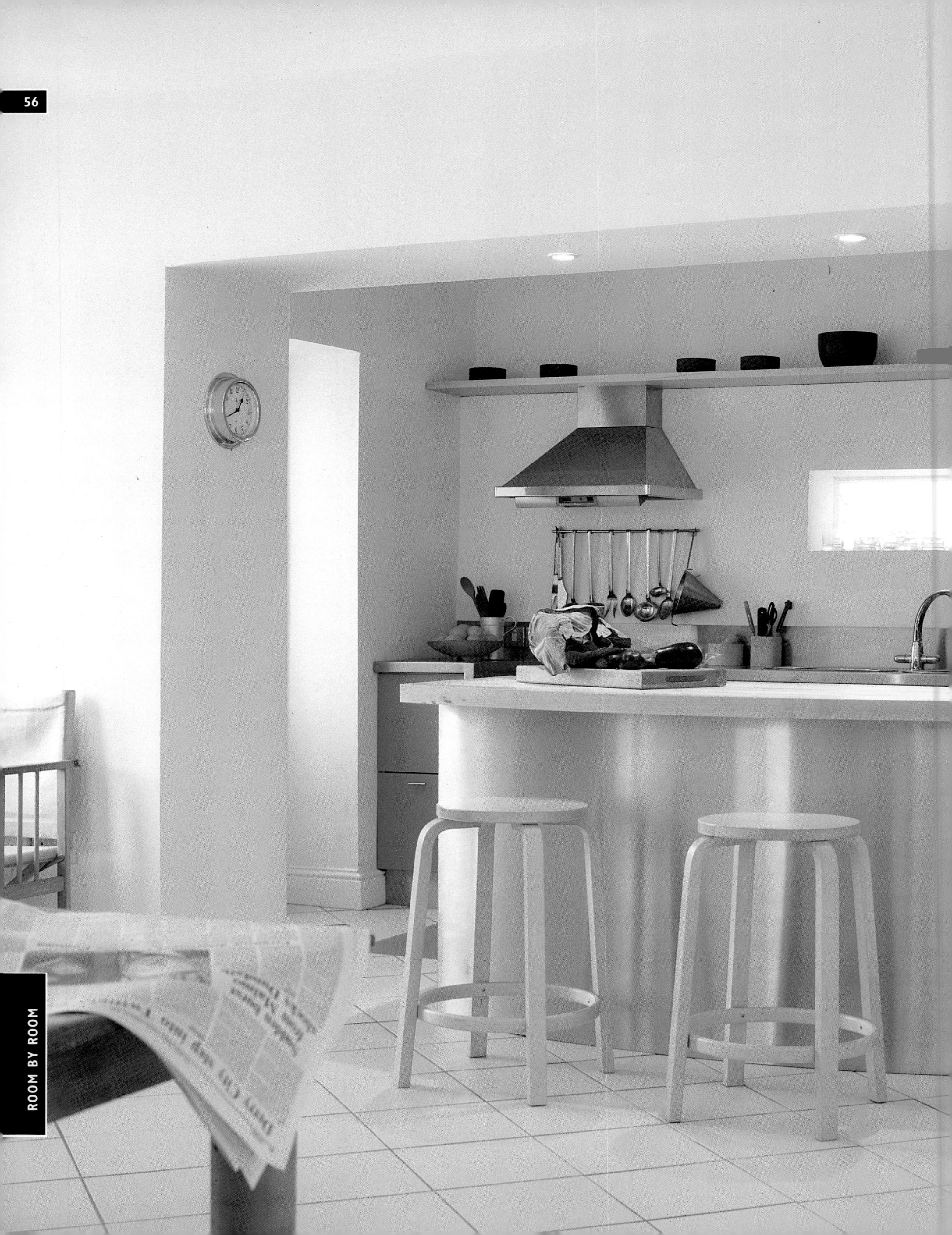

The kitchen has been restored to its rightful place at the centre of family life; no longer is it simply the place where meals are prepared. Cooking is now an everyday pleasure for many people, rather than a chore. Our social structure is more relaxed, so we invite guests to join us here for a coffee or a meal, rather than in the more formal living or dining rooms. Televisions, CDs and books are just as likely to find their way into the kitchen as the other communal areas of the house. All this elevates it to more than just a room in which to prepare food. Before you consider its storage needs, you must first think carefully about how you use your kitchen and how you would like to improve it. Good design and careful planning can open up a whole new range of possibilities. Now is the time for some decisions – are you going to work with what you have already, or are you going to begin again from scratch? Take a long hard look at how efficiently your kitchen works in terms of the three key zones: cooking, food preparation and food storage. Function is the priority here, although too often kitchens are bought and sold on their aesthetic qualities. Looks are not enough – you need a kitchen that will be the heart-beat of your home.

As with other areas of the house, the first and most essential step is to sort your kitchen paraphernalia into three piles: things you use on an everyday basis; things you hardly ever use; and things you never use. The last category might include chipped china that you never got around to repairing or wedding presents that you never liked — this pile should be disposed of or given to a charity shop or younger member of the family who could make use of these things. The second pile, which might include gadgets you rarely use or a dinner service only brought out at Christmas, should be packed away into the more inaccessible places, such as on the top of kitchen cabinets or in the basement. The first pile is the one we are concerned with here. Divide this pile according to function: all cooking implements together; all eating ones; all cleaning ones; and so on. Using the storage you have, plus a few strategic additions, you are going to find a home for each item as appropriate to its role as the cutlery tray is to the fork. With some items, this will be obvious: pan racks are for pans, knife blocks are for knives. However, for other bits and pieces — the ones that have always seemed to float from drawer to drawer — a more determined approach is needed.

Before going out and buying new accessories for an existing kitchen, take a fresh look at its architectural possibilities. Make a note of those things that are fixed and cannot be moved and those that could be. Maybe you have a piece of furniture elsewhere in the house that you could put to better use in the kitchen — a dresser (hutch), for example, offers lots of space for china, while a utility cart is ideal for storing canned goods. Ask yourself whether the cupboard space is being used effectively. What about wall space, ceiling space and floor space? Which do you have plenty of, and which are already packed tight to bursting point? Perhaps there are ways of distributing the kitchenware in a more balanced way to create a more efficient, uncluttered atmosphere?

Opposite top *Customize existing furniture to suit your needs with holders, pockets and bands.*
Opposite bottom *Simple, glazed doors protect possessions from dust, but allow you to see in.*
Left *Purpose-built open shelves make it easy to separate groups of cooking utensils.*
Top *Compact and convenient: open shelves are packed tight with essential foodstuffs.*
Above *Giant pull-out cupboards are particularly useful for bulky items.*

Good design is essential if you are really going to enjoy cooking and entertaining in the kitchen. Professionals talk about 'the triangle', which is an invisible line drawn between the three activity zones: water supply, cooking area and food storage. Each of these should be a self-contained unit with its own storage space. For safety reasons, you should try to avoid through-traffic between the stove and sink and, if possible, each area should be linked to the next, so that you can reach what you want without continually walking backwards and forwards. That is why large kitchens are not necessarily better than small ones – professional cooks will often argue that it is better to work in a small space where every item is accessible. If you have a large kitchen which you plan to use for other activities, be it chatting to friends or overseeing the children's homework, then you would do better to keep these areas separate from the cooking zone.

When considering the layout of a kitchen, you must always assess it both vertically and horizontally. There are five layouts common to most kitchens:

The single-line kitchen, where appliances and cupboards are lined against one wall – ideal where space is limited.

The galley kitchen, where appliances and units are arranged along two facing walls – the sink and stove should be on the same side.

The L-shaped kitchen, where two adjoining walls are fitted with cupboards and appliances – often seen in small, square rooms.

The U-shaped kitchen, where three of the walls are utilized, giving uninterrupted food preparation space.

The island kitchen, where space allows for a central unit – the island can also double as a room divider.

You also have the choice between fitted kitchen furniture and free-standing. This is a matter of personal taste, as each has its own advantages. Fitted units make use of available space, both in terms of the room and the interior layout of the cupboards. Free-standing kitchens have more character, and can be taken with you if you move. Your choice will also be influenced by the style of your chosen kitchen: natural or rustic, industrial or minimalist.

Once you've decided on the basic layout, you must tackle certain questions: where to install appliances such as the stove, dishwasher and fridge; which work surface to choose; what cooking equipment you need; how many sinks to include and how to create enough storage space.

Opposite top In this spacious apartment, one wall of the U-shaped kitchen acts as a divider between cooking and eating zones.

Opposite bottom The streamlined galley makes the most of corridor-type space and is very practical from a cook's point of view.

Above left The eclectic look is individual and offers flexibility as many items are free-standing.

Top The irregularity of the walls has been made into a feature with custom-made surfaces.

Above A more conventional look is the classic L-shaped layout, which is both compact and practical.

Top One of the fundamental questions when planning a kitchen is whether to conceal or display. This isn't just a question of solid or glazed doors, fitted cupboards or open shelves – here, roll-down blinds screen kitchen utensils and equipment from view for a clean, streamlined effect which looks fabulous in this industrial-style kitchen.

Above *In contrast, this simple, open shelving houses a homely collection of glasses and china. The background colour 'frames' the arrangement and draws the eye in. Remember, though, that the maintenance time for such areas is high.*

Y our kitchen storage should be planned around the appropriate zone, be it cooking, food storage or sink. The items used more frequently should be the most accessible. If you do have the opportunity to design the kitchen from scratch, then pay attention to the layout of cupboard interiors. Among the great space-wasters in the kitchen are poorly positioned shelves within cabinets – standard dimensions are installed with no real thought to the individual. If you are starting from scratch, write down a list of items to be stored and the headroom they require. Uniform depth is just as irritating – all that crashing around trying to find the right pan lid or mixing bowl. Ideally, shelves above eye level should graduate in depth, so that you can always reach to the back. If necessary, invest in a set of fold-away steps to help you reach the highest corners. Lower-level units can incorporate all manner of pull-out trays, bins and carousels. Take this one step further and install shelf dividers to create narrow compartments where you can keep slim-line bakeware. Swing-out racks increase the storage space available, particularly in corner units; so do narrow shelves built inside cupboard doors.

Don't despair if you can't afford a new kitchen. There are many commercially available fittings that can transform the efficiency of a kitchen – from baskets to fit inside shelves to a rack at the back of the work surface on which to hang utensils. Unit doors are cheap to replace if you want to create a new style or colour scheme. If you have the skills to refit

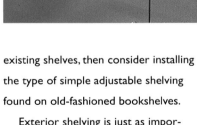

existing shelves, then consider installing the type of simple adjustable shelving found on old-fashioned bookshelves.

Exterior shelving is just as important. Think hard about varying the height of shelves depending on what is to be stored there – be it books, spices or CDs to play while you work. You might want to keep some things at a high level out of reach of children, but provide low-level shelving for their books, paints and cassettes.

TIPS

- Invest in a bin with separate compartments to recycle glass and foodstuffs. Crush cans and flatten packets.
- Use airtight containers for storing foodstuffs to keep out bugs.
- Keep a shopping master list and arrange items in categories.
- File magazine recipes immediately, and organize by types of dishes or by particular cooks.
- When following a recipe, weigh out and organize everything in advance, and jot down key stages on a sticker.
- Keep herbs and spices clearly on view, either face up in a drawer or in small wire baskets.
- Use ice-cube trays to freeze sauces in individual portions.
- For dinner parties, lay the table and arrange flowers in the morning.

Above *Most kitchens offer a combination of 'hide and display' storage. Custom-built furniture has the advantage of being designed with very specific items in mind – such as this collection of bowls. Less attractive items can be hidden away behind closed doors, with just one or two pieces – such as this lemon squeezer – left on view. Cupboards of different heights and widths are essential because they take into account the different scale of your possessions. If possible, try to include some with variable depth so that slimline goods don't always find their way to the inaccessible back.*

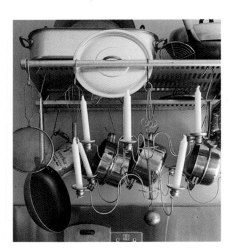

Top *A simple, accessible shelving system is useful for separating tableware into like-with-like groups.*

Above *Hanging racks like this are ideal in tight corners. Even the chandelier has a home.*

Right *In a large kitchen, you can find yourself wearing out the soles of your shoes endlessly walking from one set of cupboards to another. A trolley (cart) is a practical solution because it doubles both as storage space and work surface.*

Far right *Don't forget the vertical space at the back of work surfaces for kitchen utensils you use on a regular basis.*

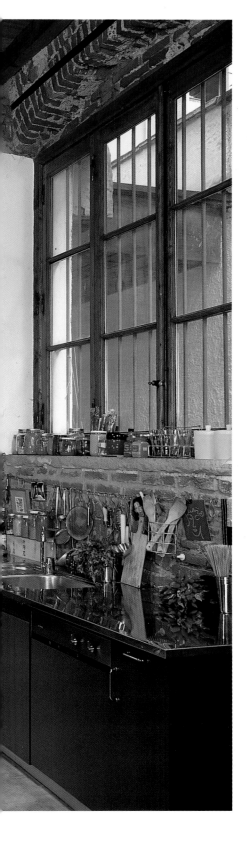

Cooking is at the heart of the kitchen, even if you spend more time heating up take-aways than turning your hand to cordon bleu. Your cooking appliances will help determine what sort of storage you need for cooking utensils, but as with other areas this will depend largely on whether you want to display or conceal.

In a modern, streamlined kitchen with built-in stove, you might prefer to tuck pots and pans away in nearby cupboards – perhaps the stove even has a pan drawer. But in a kitchen with a cast-iron range, you might choose to draw the eye towards it and make a display of heavy-bottomed cast iron or copper pans. There are plenty of attractive pan racks for this purpose, including ceiling racks with butcher's hooks and free-standing pot stands. Big, bulky pots and pans are easy to find no matter how crowded the kitchen is, but flat cookware items are another matter – baking loses its appeal when you've

wasted ten minutes hunting for the appropriate cookie sheet or muffin pan. These sorts of items, as well as pan lids, are best kept together in a tall, wire unit where you can see exactly what you have, and where they won't come tumbling out every time you open the cupboard door. Don't store such things up high – a hurt foot is better than a cracked skull!

Think about what you actually use when cooking. Do you need wooden spoons handy? Oven gloves? Kitchen towel? Recipe books? Salt and pepper? Is there a surface nearby where you can put down heavy, hot pans? There is no need to have every appliance you own on display, so if, for example, your pasta machine or ice-cream maker is used fairly rarely, then it makes sense to put it at a high level out of sight. Do keep all the accessories together, though – there's nothing more frustrating than getting the food processor out and then spending 15 minutes hunting for the right blade.

Above *Kitchen cupboard interiors have become ever more inventive, with carousels at every corner and a spectacular assortment of flip-down, pull-up, slide-out extras making it possible to utilize every bit of space.*

Right *The space under the sink is usually where cleaning products and pet food gather, but there is no reason why you shouldn't put it to more imaginative use.*

Bottom right *The old-fashioned butler's sink with plate rack above is making a comeback because it combines both function and aesthetics. This one has been custom-built to complement the Georgian architecture of the house.*

Bottom far right *You can find a shelf to suit any style of kitchen – wire mesh is strong and allows pans to drain as they stand.*

When it comes to planning out the sink area, first think about all the activities you use yours for: washing dishes, soaking clothes, preparing vegetables, rinsing food, arranging flowers, filling up the kettle, children's creative play, bathing the dog and so on. What do you need handy to carry out these activities, and which of them take priority? Take this one step further and ask yourself what sort of items you want on display and what you would like to conceal.

Old-fashioned plate racks have made a comeback in recent years. Not only are they functional, particularly if placed over the sink, but they also make an attractive display area (as long as the plates are fairly uniform in style) and cut down on the drying-up. If you are having a kitchen custom-built and a plate rack is an option, make sure the maker has a sample of your own china so that the plates fit securely. In terms of storage, most people opt to display their most attractive cups, jugs, coffeepots and so on, and to conceal those that are not so covetable.

If you have a dishwasher, you will probably find it tempting to store everyday tableware there, but the organized cook should always ensure it's unloaded after use. Slimline models are ideal for one or two people as it's a waste of energy to run a larger machine when only a quarter full.

In a house with no dishwasher, two sinks are definitely better than one. Decide which is to be used for washing dirty plates and which is for food preparation, then plan the surrounding storage space around these activities. The washing-up sink needs a place for cleaning products, dishcloths and tea towels, not to mention a drainage area for wet dishes and a rubbish bin for plate scrapings. The food preparation sink needs an empty work surface for foods, plus a space for all the gadgetry associated with preparing it – knives, peelers, pans, chopping boards and so on. Look closely at the areas below, above and around your sinks. Below the sink is the obvious place for unsightly

things like cleaning products and pet food; above the sink is more suited to plate racks and display cabinets; and the surrounding worktop is the most useful site for cooking utensils.

Flick through home-interest magazines and you'll find them bursting with all sorts of practical and economical ways of dealing with kitchen clutter – from pull-out metal baskets for cleaning products to multi-purpose dispensers for dustcloths and carrier bags.

Food, after all, is what the kitchen is all about. Cooking is more of a pleasure if you are organized, in terms of both time and making sure you can find what you need. Divide food storage into essentials, usefuls and luxuries, bearing in mind that different foods need different conditions: dried foodstuffs, cookies, sugars and flours, for example, last longest at room temperature, while fruit, vegetables and wine are best kept in a cool, dark spot. If your kitchen wall cupboards have under-unit lighting, beware: lights heat up surrounding surfaces and your groceries will quickly perish. If you're lucky enough to have an old-fashioned pantry in the kitchen, then make the most of it. The modern refrigerator was never a proper substitute for the spacious, cool and well-ventilated pantry.

That's not to underestimate the value of fridges and freezers. Choose the largest you can accommodate and buy stackable models if space is a problem. Chest freezers take up lots of floor space, so they are best restricted to a utility room or garage in a household that needs a large amount of food. Vertical freezers take up less room and have the advantage that you can see exactly what you have – most have separate drawers for storing meat, fish, vegetables and so on. Freezers run more economically when kept well stocked.

When freezing, remember the importance of labelling – you need to know both what you have frozen and when. If there are only one or two of you in the household, there's no point in freezing large quantities. If you do buy in bulk, divide your food into portions and place it in freezer bags. Sterilized jars are ideal for small quantities of soups, sauces and the like. When packing your freezer, try to keep like with like, and have a good clear-out now and then to make sure nothing has been left buried at the bottom.

If you're short on pantry or cupboard space, a utility cart on castors is a good investment for canned and packaged food. Not only can you stack it as deep as you want, but it also comes in handy when you're unpacking the groceries, as you can pull it as close to the bags as you need. These carts come in all sizes and styles – from heavy-duty industrial designs to old-fashioned rustic versions.

Bulky food buys, such as large quantities of pet food or cases of soft drinks, should be placed as high out of view as possible. Or explore the possibility of creating a food storage space out of stackable drawers, including jumbo-sized ones.

Not everything needs to be hidden away inside cupboards. Some foods are attractive in their own right and many are packaged with this in mind: vinegars, oils and preserves, for example. Remember to throw things out when they're past their prime and keep perishables out of the sun. Buy baskets and bowls for fruit; hang fresh herbs or dried chillies from ceiling racks; display home-pickled wares on open shelves; and have strings of onions and garlic hanging near the cooking zone.

Opposite top *Industrial shelving is strong and flexible. Here, it has been softened with the addition of giant baskets and plain glass jars chosen to complement and display the wares.*

Left *Food with the feel-good factor — bright colours, generous-sized bowls and colourful jars combine to create a party atmosphere. The bead curtains are a stimulating alternative to solid unit doors, and are, of course, cheaper too.*

Above *Open shelves of varying heights have been packed tight with matching glass storage jars for all the essential foodstuffs — compact and convenient.*

DINING AREAS

I f your kitchen is large enough to take a sizeable table, the chances are that you will end up eating there a lot of the time. You can either choose to make the table the focal point of the room – a place for guests to sit and chat while you cook – or you can isolate it from the rest of the room by creating a partition with kitchen base units or even folding screens. As with other areas of the kitchen, you want to have the essentials easily accessible, so china, glasses, linen, candles and cutlery should all be stored nearby.

Sideboards might seem old-fashioned today, but they serve their purpose well: they offer storage space for eating implements; their surface is ideal for carving meat or slicing fish; and salads, bread, fruit and cheese can all be displayed there until required. Maybe you have another piece of furniture that will serve the same purpose – a dresser (hutch), perhaps, or old-fashioned chiffonier? If you are proud of your china and glasses and want to display them, then some form of open shelving is called for: perhaps you need a dresser top to match the base mentioned previously? China that is for display purposes only should be placed as high up as possible – on custom-built shelves, for example, with a lip to stop it falling.

Cutlery should also be stored properly: you can buy everyday knives and forks with a holder on which they hang, but good-quality silver should be stored in velvet-lined boxes to prevent tarnishing. If you've got the space, a trolley (cart) with wheels is highly practical, particularly if you like to eat al fresco.

Opposite *A dining area that leads from the kitchen is the ideal arrangement for most people. Choose furniture that integrates with both areas: this simple trolley (cart) is an attractive side table and makes laying the table and clearing away again easier.*
Above *Few people have the luxury of a dining area that is used exclusively for eating – most double as work surfaces or study areas. This enormous storage cabinet is an ideal place to bundle all the 'extras' of family life – books, tapes, toys and so on – when you clear the table for its original purpose.*
Right *In contrast, minimalism reigns in this stream-lined dining room, where built-in cabinets line the walls keeping clutter out of sight. It's an uncompromising approach that not everyone can live with.*

EXTRAS

Of course there are other items, some of them unattractive and bulky, that also need a home in the kitchen: the ironing board, mop, broom, bucket and vacuum cleaner to name a few. A tall cupboard is an effective way of storing these, but don't cram it so full that everything comes tumbling out when you open the door. Fix hooks on the inside walls to hang dustcloths and brooms, and include a special container for things like vacuum cleaner accessories. For convenience sake, make sure the door can swing right back to give you as much room as possible – you don't always want to be pushing and squeezing things through narrow gaps. An interior light is also useful.

Often the kitchen is the most frequently used room in the house, the centre of family life. What else do you use yours for: crafts, homework, watching television, doing the household accounts, cleaning shoes? Whatever the activity, you must think about where you are going to store things when not in use. This doesn't necessarily mean providing a lot of space – a drawer or shelf might suffice. Children's art materials, for example, might be kept in a colourful plastic carton; knitting wools could have a home in a pretty wicker basket; homework in a particular drawer; and newspapers on a wooden tray. The secret is to make sure you use the allotted space for that activity only and don't clutter it up with other unnecessary junk.

Because of the proximity to water, the kitchen might even double as your craft studio. In that case, you must store your

materials away from foodstuffs and make sure everything is easy to clean and put away when you've finished a project. Utility carts, portable plastic baskets and sturdy boxes all offer excellent storage solutions.

Utility rooms

The idea of separating the kitchen into zones is a lot easier if you also have a utility room where laundry equipment, fridge, dishwasher and all the other bulky and ugly appliances that kitchens attract can be stored away. Dedicated storage rooms don't have to have the same aesthetic appeal as other rooms, but they should be well organized. Plan out how you're going to get the most from your utility area. Think about what equipment you need to store there, what activities you will be doing and whether you have enough surfaces. In any case, a separate sink is an excellent idea, but once again you have to decide how it is to be used

Left One end of the family kitchen in this spacious Victorian house has been commandeered for creative activities. You might not have this option, but a big table, practical flooring and drawer space for pens and paper can fulfil the same function.

Below Think about all the activities that go on in the kitchen and how to make them as enjoyable as possible – if ironing is a chore, why not lighten the load with a television or CD player?

Bottom This combination of sofa, dining table, television and book shelves is typical of a contemporary approach to the heart of the house.

most efficiently and what needs to be located nearby. Perhaps you will also keep bulk supplies of household goods here, or craft equipment? If you are environmentally aware, this might be the place where you sort and store goods for recycling. In other words, the utility room is not the poor relation to the kitchen, but a valuable work room in its own right. Take a fresh look at yours and try to find ways of improving its efficiency by making better use of floor, wall or ceiling space.

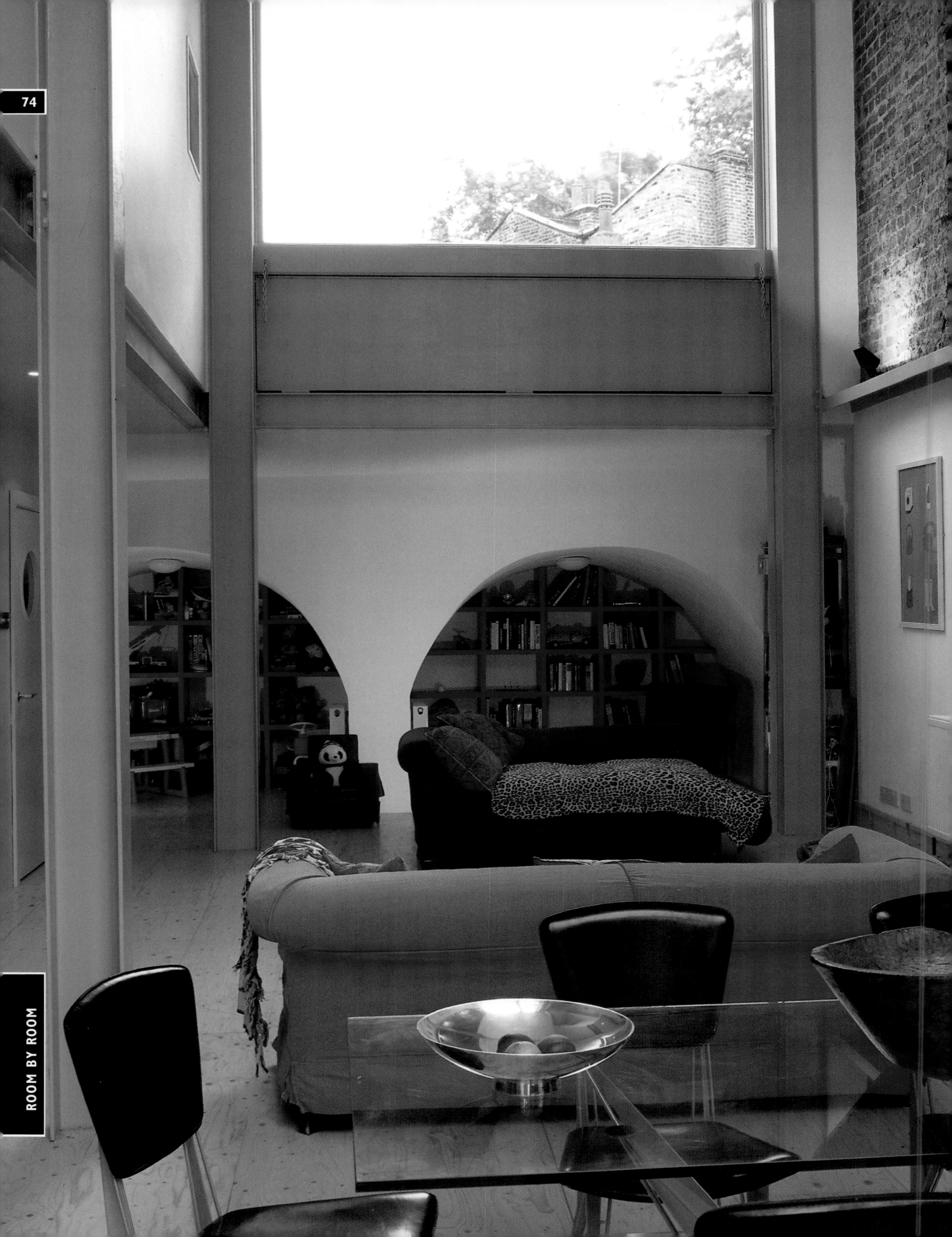

LIVING ROOMS

The living room is the nerve centre of the household. It is here that adults and children flop down at the end of a long, hard day; it is here that they congregate to talk, to read or simply to relax. But the living room is more than just the main communal space, it is also where guests are entertained. That means it has to cope both with your personal needs and your public face. Creating a successful living space isn't just about providing comfortable chairs and a stimulating colour scheme – it's also about making sure the design works at every level, and for everyone who uses it. Living rooms have so many different functions, you must begin by assessing what these are: being with friends, watching television, reading, sewing, practising the piano, playing games, talking on the phone. Don't forget other members of the household as you will need to make space for their toys, CD collections, homework, hobbies and so on. Consider whether any of these can be siphoned off to other areas of the house – maybe it's possible to create a study area elsewhere, or move the television into the kitchen? Once you've come up with a definitive list, consider how well it serves its purpose and whether there is room for improvement.

No-one would dream of designing a kitchen without drawing up a scaled plan first, but it's surprising how few people follow this concept through to other areas of the house. Yet in the living room, it makes perfect sense. Mark out doors, windows and any permanent features, such as fireplaces, built-in cupboards and power points, and then think about the areas you need to create within this framework. Obviously seating will be the first priority, and the chances are that this will relate to the siting of the television. Measure your furniture and cut out paper shapes in scale with your drawing – you can try out all sorts of layouts on paper that you might never have considered when standing in the room. Also mark out traffic routes across the room, such as from the door to the sofa or from the sofa to the CD player. A lot of people will be using this room, and they must be able to do so easily and safely. Once you've decided on the layout of the room, you can tackle your storage requirements.

The first thing you must decide is whether to keep existing storage furniture or buy something new. If you're working to a tight budget, you probably want to avoid buying new pieces, but it's worth reassessing existing furniture – for example, you might have a linen press or ottoman in the bedroom that would be twice as useful in the living room. We all get very set in our ways, but why not take this opportunity to move things around and create a fresh look?

Space allowing, you should include at least one large-scale shelving unit in your plan – this might be a modern chrome-and-glass cabinet or a traditional solid wood bookcase. Whatever its style, it will be one of the main features of the room, so choose it with care.

Buying old pieces of furniture is nearly always cheaper than buying new, and you can take pride in owning something both original and attractive. Don't worry if it's not in perfect condition as you might want

Far left In a tiny space, such as this intimate reading corner, it's important to choose furniture that serves more than one function. Chairs are placed next to this honeycomb-style storage unit so that the shelves can be used as a table surface for the occasional coffee cup, as well as being a permanent home for collections of magazines and decorative items. The magazines are catalogued by title and kept in orderly, chronological piles so that particular issues can be found easily.
Left At one end of an enormous living room is a bold dining area-cum-office. A bank of filing

cabinets provides valuable storage, and also accentuates the hard lines of the room. It's an extreme example of how to make the most of available wall space, leaving the floor clear and uncluttered.
Above This minimalist interior has taken the bare essentials of the living room – a table and seating – and, by removing everything else, made them the focus of the space. Such an approach relies partly on having somewhere to conceal all your things, and partly on having few things to conceal in the first place. It demands a purist's eye and absolute discipline in maintaining the look.

to customize the interior anyway to make room for, say, your music centre or videos.

There are plenty of antique pieces that look at home in contemporary living rooms: old medicine cabinets are perfect for housing all manner of household items from balls of string and staplers to passports and postcards; coffers provide a home for magazines and newspapers; old trunks can double as coffee tables; and display cabinets can show off anything from silver spoons to fishing lures.

If antique furniture isn't your style, there are many contemporary designs to choose from. The cheapest option is to choose those you assemble yourself; if you buy modular systems you can add to them when your possessions dictate. You won't be able to enjoy the beauty of solid wood, but the laminated boards from which most are constructed come in a wide range of finishes and many are suitable for painting. If you're furnishing your home from scratch, try not to make rash decisions based on aesthetics alone. Instead, think about how well a piece of furniture will serve the function you require and whether it will fit into the overall scale of the room. Manufacturers' catalogues give dimensions, so there's no need to rely on luck.

Built-in pieces of furniture with customized interiors are the most expensive option, but a sensible one in a small living room that has to fulfil many functions. If you inherit someone else's built-in furniture, think twice before ripping it out, no matter how ugly it is. You might be able to hang on to the interior storage and change the exterior so that it's more in keeping with your taste. Perhaps you could replace the doors, or paint and stencil them to give them a new lease of life?

Some form of shelving is another essential, but first decide whether to display or conceal your possessions. Most people prefer a half-and-half solution because books, photographs, flowers and ornaments add some interest and character to a house, whereas unsightly wires and hi-tech black boxes do not. This is all a matter of personal choice, and the style of the room should dictate what you expose and what you choose to cover up. When building new shelves yourself, take care that you position them well as far as safety is concerned – no-one will thank you if you fix them so high that they keep banging their heads on them.

If you have alcoves in your living room, perhaps on either side of the fireplace, you might choose to build shelves or cabinets into these spaces – either low-level ones or floor-to-ceiling. Well positioned cupboards can hide unsightly radiators and provide an ordered look to the room.

Opposite Simplicity is the key to this creamy sanctuary. A witty touch is provided on the canvas screens that shroud the bookcases – hand-drawn sketches of shelves and books that give a clue to what lies inside. A junkshop table is elevated to something grander with the use of a good linen cloth and carefully placed accessories.

Right Understairs space needn't mean a utility cupboard or toilet. Here, it has been opened up to provide extra shelf space and room for a compact daybed. Small spaces can actually appear larger when crammed with furniture and possessions.

Comfortable sofas and chairs are a priority in the living room, but what will people be doing when they sit there? Watching television, knitting, reading magazines? What will they need to carry out these activities?

The most obvious requirement will be a table of some description. Perhaps this will have a shelf ledge underneath which can double the surface area? A hard, durable surface will prove most useful for hot cups of coffee and the like. Stackable tables are an excellent choice because they can be hidden away when not in use. If there's no room for a table, you will need to fix shelves at a convenient height near to the seating area.

In a living room that also doubles as a dining room, there might be one large table that fulfils many needs: the focus for family meals, entertaining friends, doing homework or cutting out dress patterns. You will need specific storage for all these functions – a sideboard is the obvious place for tableware, glasses and cutlery, but you might also need shelves or cupboards for other items like needlework, writing paper, toys, board games or reference books.

Storage is not just about large pieces of furniture, but about small containers too. Everything you use should have a home of its own and this should be chosen to suit the scale of the items it is going to house. Baskets, jars, boxes and tins are perfect for storing the various pieces that make up the jigsaw of life in the living room and all of these have the advantage of being portable. Remember the golden rule –

store like with like – and you will never have difficulty finding anything again. By choosing with care, you can make these containers an interesting feature of the room in their own right – especially if you pick ones that tie in with the interior design, be it natural vegetable-dyed baskets for newspapers, chic metal tins for CDs, funky plastic boxes for toys or antique wooden chests for board games. They need not cost the earth and can be added to over time.

Below In this compact apartment, seating signifies where each zone starts and finishes – not just the obvious dining and sitting areas, but also the reading corner on the upper level. Cupboards under the raised platform provide concealed storage.
Right Stackable butterfly chairs are a useful buy if you need a certain amount of flexibility.
Far right Space is precious in this tiny mews house, so furniture has been chosen for its portability as much for its visual style. A black-bordered rug signifies the division between dining and sitting areas, while a sliding door screens the bed.

TIPS

- Make displays of functional as well as decorative things such as beautiful drinking glasses or serving dishes.
- Allow yourself one week's worth of papers and magazines, and then recycle. Cut out and keep articles of interest.
- For built-in storage systems, choose a joiner whose style is in sympathy with your home. Ask to see photographs of previous work.

- If you are looking for an antique bookcase or cabinet, carry the dimensions around with you when scanning auctions and junkshops.
- Number your videos and keep a list of them, organized alphabetically, by title, director or genre.
- Have an annual clear-out of your CD and record collections and keep only your favourites.

In many houses, the television is the focus of the living room and seating is arranged to give everyone the best possible view. Even if it's concealed in a cabinet or a table, it will be obvious at a glance where it is because of this.

The television is usually partnered by the video recorder and a stack of videos. Perhaps, for convenience sake, these are situated near the hi-fi, CD player and music collection. All of these need power points, and that means trailing wires and even radio aerials. In other words, a mess.

You have a choice of approaches. The first is to revel in your electronic hardware and make it a feature in its own right. Select a wall situated close to the seating area and create a custom-made unit to house it all. Design this so that it offers the potential to take an ever-expanding collection of videos, CDs and computer games. Modular systems are available in endless combinations, offering versatile storage that can be extended or amended to suit your needs. An alternative approach is to create a rather more

integrated look by separating certain components of your home leisure collection. Obviously the television must be seen, but could the video recorder, CD player, amplifier and radio be hidden elsewhere in the room? Perhaps the wires that connect them can be run at a high level – for example, you could tack them onto the picture rail, if there is one, so that they are not noticed. Speakers must be placed where they have optimum effect, but don't draw attention to them by placing pot plants or other ornaments on top – this has the opposite effect to the one you intend by drawing the eye towards the object you are trying to conceal.

You can buy free-standing furniture and screens designed to hide the television, but consider whether this is really necessary. Perhaps you could trade yours in for a smaller, less obtrusive model, or you could rearrange the furniture slightly so that it doesn't point quite so obviously to where the television is? Make a focal point of something else in the room like the fireplace or a particularly fine painting.

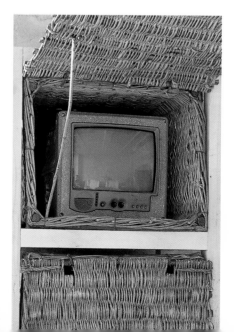

Opposite Few living rooms escape the presence of a television, but that doesn't mean it has to be the focal point. Here, seating is grouped in such a way that the view is taken first to the glass-topped table and then out to the garden. There's no attempt to hide the home-leisure equipment, but it doesn't dominate.

Left and far left Solutions for hiding the television range from the natural-looking to the chic.

Top Flat items can be stored in slimline baskets or boxes that complement their scale.

Above An amusing interpretation of a mobile music centre – the tapes are kept on custom-made shelves.

In a family household, the living room often doubles up as a playroom too. Young children like to be near adults and for safety's sake this is the best place for them. Don't fight the invasion of toys, games and books – learn to deal with it. It makes sense to allocate a corner of the room that is recognizably theirs and this will prevent toys from encroaching on the rest of the room. You might even include a small-scale table and set of chairs, so that eating and drinking as well as drawing and modelling can be enjoyed there. If you want your children to clear up after playtime, make sure shelves and drawers are placed within their reach. If you provide enough storage for all their needs, they will feel much more inclined to tidy up. Low-level shelving or cupboards are ideal for storing boxes of toys, but you will also need to create a permanent home for books and games.

The key to success is to introduce a simple system early on that your child can understand. Provide a container for every type of toy and make sure they are always put away properly at the end of the day – with your help, of course. If you make it clear that farm animals always go in, say, the blue box and building bricks in the red one, you will be teaching your child an important lesson for life – that the way to start any successful storage system is to store like with like. Of course, there won't always be time to be so disciplined – if all the toys end up tipped into one box, that's OK: just make sure you don't let them leave it that way for too long.

If you really don't want to see children's clutter when you're enjoying adult company in the evening, then buy enough attractive containers to hide it away. Large wicker laundry baskets are ideal, as are antique coffers (so long as you add safety catches to protect little fingers). Or buy a utility cart on castors, so that you can simply pack everything up in the evening and wheel it right out of sight.

As children get older, they don't feel the need to be with you all the time but, surprisingly, their possessions do. Trainers, comics, school projects and discarded T-shirts all seem to gravitate towards the living room. How you react to this depends on what sort of parent you are and how you plan to deal with it long-term. In the short term, you need a hide-all of some description, like a chest or ottoman. But make a rule that it's emptied out completely at least once a week or the contents will be thrown away. There is no harm in trying to teach the basic principle of communal living – that no-one has to live with someone else's junk.

Right *A former cellar has been converted into a generous-sized family room. Arches make natural divisions, and the owners have made features of these by allocating one to adults and one to children. It's the ideal solution – the youngsters have an area that's recognizably theirs with shelves for toys, a chair to sit on and a washable floor that can withstand wear and tear. Adults have a corner in which to escape with a cup of coffee and a book, but from where they're able to supervise the activities 'next door'. Children enjoy privacy and the coziness of this niche is similar to that of a playhouse.*

Above *This high-level home office is the ideal way of integrating a desk into a living room – it is part of the space, yet away from it. The cupboard underneath takes most of the overflow of everyday living, and is an ideal way of utilizing the area created by a raised platform. The tall carousel is an ingenious addition – it again makes the most of vertical space, but also provides a link from lower to upper storeys. Shallow, low-level storage is concealed behind the wooden panels which line the room – pictures are not hung on the wall but propped on the shelf.*

Perhaps one of you has to work in the living room, either on the computer or sorting out household accounts at a small desk. Obviously, as a communal area this isn't the best place in the house to choose, but maybe you do have it to yourself during the day when everyone is out at work or school.

Choose the quietest corner you can, well away from the television or music system. Make sure you have enough light

and that there are power points close by. The most basic requirements are a desk or table to work on and somewhere to store all your paperwork. As this is a communal space, you should opt for storage that allows you to put everything right out of sight at the end of your working day. Perhaps you could manage with just a few shelves above the desk – if it's in an alcove, you could use pull-down blinds to screen it off when not in use. Try to avoid

furniture that's obviously designed for an office, such as metal filing cabinets. This corner is only one area of the room and must co-ordinate with the space as a whole. Choose furniture that is aesthetically pleasing, but which will also be comfortable to sit on and use. Buy pieces that also offer storage potential – deep drawers or pull-up lids, for example.

There are plenty of products on the market that allow you to sort and file

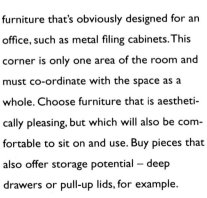

papers, without resorting to the old-fashioned cabinet. Increasingly popular are the small cabinets on wheels that can be pushed out of sight when not needed. Where possible, try to minimize the amount of paper you store – keep documents on floppy disk or store anything not used on a daily basis in another part of the house. If this is an area used by other members of the household, for homework maybe, make sure there's no chance of work getting mixed up and lost. Keep colour-coded boxes to separate various people's projects and make sure each person clears the desk or work surface completely after use. If more than one person uses the computer, introduce a similar system for storing away disks. The chances are that you will need a phone nearby – make sure there's a jotter on which messages for other members of the family can be taken.

Top Open shelves are ideal in a home office where you need to see where everything is, and there are styles to suit every home. This combination of wood and tubular steel is functional, strong and bold. Labelled boxes are used to store things not on display, and under-shelf space is also utilized.

Above This streamlined unit with plenty of shelf space and pull-out surfaces for computer keyboard or writing notes provides a neat solution. Lighting is important when working – a compact anglepoise lamp clipped to a shelf takes up minimum room.

LIVING ROOMS

The living room is also a public space, where your things are on display. If you have a collection of anything – from toy cars to coffeepots, paperbacks to decorative eggs – then this is the natural room in which to display it.

The secret with any collection is to create a unified look, which means displaying your prized possessions en masse rather than dispersing them throughout the house; any group of similar objects has an impact that individual items lose.

Think first about where to site the collection – do you want it at a high level out of reach of curious little fingers? Do you want to protect it behind glass or keep it away from sunlight? Do you have an alcove or other niche that needs filling? Or are you planning to commission a special piece of furniture to house it in? Open shelves are the cheapest option and can also be the most effective. Rather than spending money on a custom-made display unit, you may do better to opt for shelves

and spend the money you have saved on lighting them really well – glass in particular is greatly enhanced with the right lighting. Colour is also a consideration – the background colour you choose should not compete for attention with the collection itself, but should draw the eye towards it. Next time you visit a museum, study the use of colour and lighting.

Don't neglect wall space. Flat objects, such as old menus or matchboxes, take on new life when framed in complementary groups. The only rule is that you must keep your collection clean – grimy pottery or tarnished silver is better out of sight than on proud display. One final word of advice: don't allow your collection to encroach on family life – if it starts to grow to gargantuan proportions, creeping over every surface and every shelf, then the time has come to edit some pieces out. Perhaps you have other areas of the house you can commandeer for display, keeping only the best for the living room?

Far left Absolutely anything can become a collection
– the trick is in grouping like items with like and displaying them in a visually stimulating way. These
heavy-duty gloves would look out of place in a display
cabinet, but pinned in rows on a white background
they look striking.

Left Sometimes a collection is dictated by the space
that needs filling; at other times it takes over and
dictates the furniture needed in which to store it.
This magnificent assortment of antique trunks is an
example of the latter. Arranged two by two in a
custom-built set of cupboards, they are prized for
their faded grandeur and for the romantic visions
they conjure up. They do of course provide useful
storage in their own right, but the owners prefer to
think of what would have been inside them rather
than fill them with today's bits and pieces.

Above If you can't afford fine art, the solution is to
buy bulk instead and make the grouping of the pictures more important than the individual ones. This
arrangement reflects the line of the stairs.

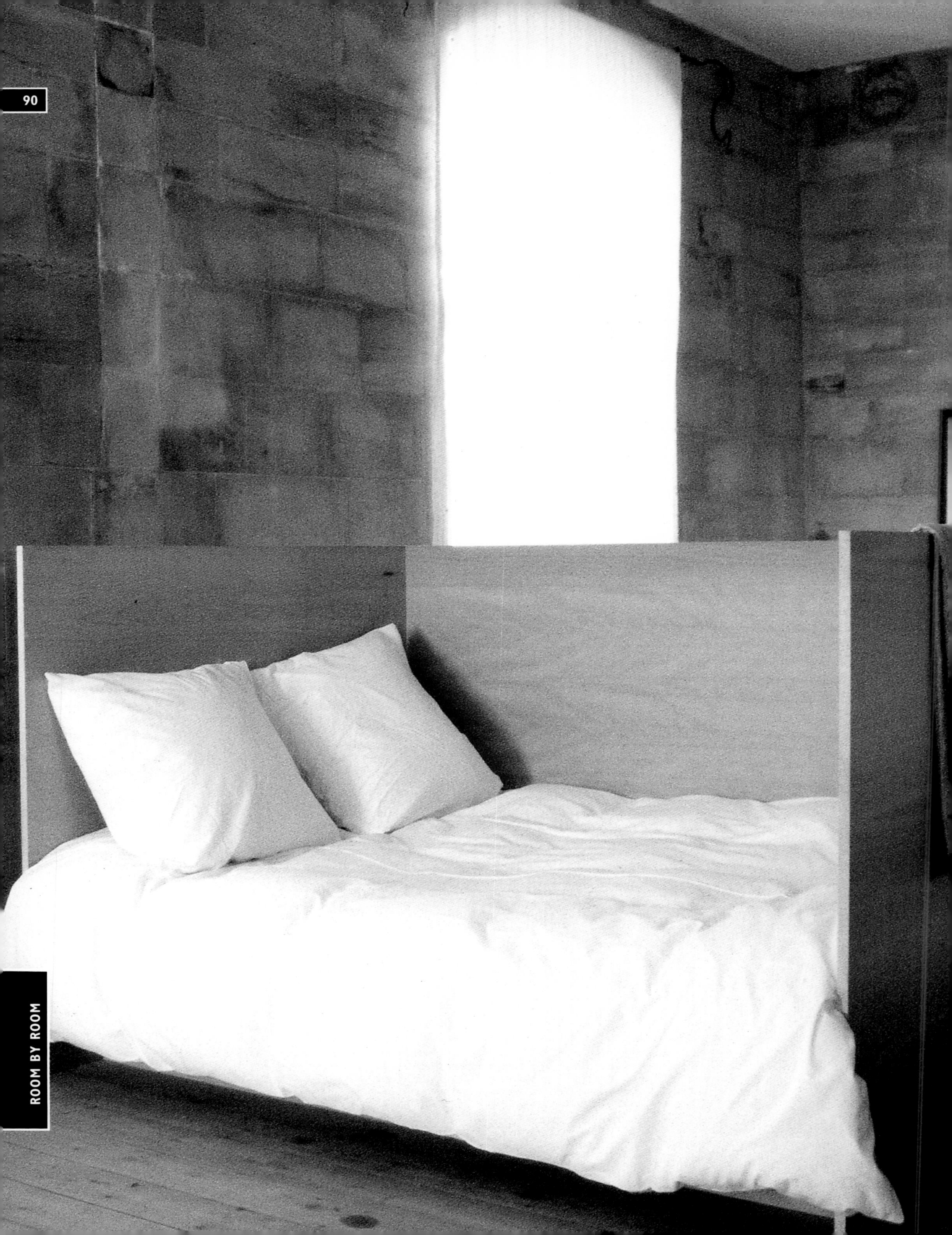

BEDROOMS

Your bedroom is the most personal room of the house – a place in which to indulge, to relax and to recover from the day's stresses. It's also the place where you keep your most intimate possessions and savour your most sensuous moments. But who wants to spend time in a room littered with dirty underwear, half-drunk mugs of coffee, last week's Sunday papers and waste baskets full of used tissues? Wise up and clean up. Your clothes and shoes need a firm hand; your bedside table needs to be blitzed; and all your drawers kicked into shape. Only then will you find peace. Easier said than done, you murmur? Easier than you think, is the answer. As with everything else, it comes down to discipline. Bedrooms are so often the places where we hoard the most – out of sight of visitors and other members of the household. The first step is to turn a critical eye on the clothes in the wardrobe, the shoes under the bed and the bits and pieces that litter every surface and fill up every drawer.

Some people eat for comfort, while others find it by surrounding themselves with all sorts of redundant things. But face up to facts – you will never find true comfort by sleeping in the middle of clutter.

Take a look at the room you have chosen as your bedroom. It may not be the biggest room in the house – perhaps you chose it for other reasons, such as its lovely view or interesting shape? Consider what you are going to use it for. Apart from sleeping in it, you may also want a haven in which to read, relax and write letters; maybe you need to work there at a computer; or perhaps you are keen to turn it into a mini gym for early-morning workouts? Who else shares this room with you and what do they use it for? Is it where you store your clothes and shoes? What else do you keep there: books, luggage, make-up, dirty linen?

Only by assessing your needs can you establish which areas need improvement. Look at the available space and make a note of any 'dead' areas that could be used more effectively. The simplest way of employing such space to the full is to build floor-to-ceiling cupboards that give you plenty of high-level storage. But if this is too expensive or not practical in an awkwardly shaped room, there are plenty of alternatives. High-level shelves are easy to erect and make perfect sense for bulky items. Under-bed storage is often overlooked, but special canvas bags and boxes on castors are designed to make the most of this space. If you dislike your existing built-in furniture, think carefully before ripping it out. No matter how ugly, if it provides good storage it makes sense to keep it. Consider painting and stencilling the exterior; replacing unsightly doors with panels; covering them with fabric; or fitting pull-down blinds in their place.

Above Make use of every corner of space by utilizing architectural features such as niches and alcoves. This window alcove has been transformed into a storage nerve-centre with the addition of custom-made drawers. A variety of widths and depths makes them even more flexible, and they can also double as a window seat.

Right Even in a small bedroom, a wall of storage can make all the difference. Here, floor-to-ceiling cupboards with well-designed interiors take a vast quantity of clothes and accessories. A small table is a useful surface for a lamp and reading material.

Top A free-standing chest-of-drawers fits snugly into a bedroom niche. Concealed lighting makes the surface as useful as the different-sized drawers. If you can't afford custom-made furniture, carry the dimensions of such spaces with you so that you can seize the opportunity to buy pieces that fit.

Above Make the most of the space under the bed – built-in drawers, such as the ones shown here, are ideal for storing linens, nightwear and other related items. If your bed doesn't come already equipped, there are plenty of commercial products that can be bought separately and do the job just as well.

Because of the nature of the things stored there, bedrooms can become untidy very quickly. As far as clothes are concerned, you need a suitable mix of hanging and folding space. A horizontal pole is the ideal place for hanging clothes, but it doesn't have to be part of a closet – a portable one as found in clothes shops can suffice. A chest-of-drawers is the obvious place for folded clothes, but again it's not the only solution: there are many commercially made stacking systems on the market that exploit space to the full. A flat surface, such as a dressing table or bedside cabinet, is a must for a lamp, telephone, book, spectacles, drinking glass, make-up and so on.

Built-in furniture is the smart solution and has the advantage that it can be custom-made to suit your requirements. The interior should offer a comprehensive range of pull-out drawers, adjustable rails, hooks and shoe racks. If the clothes you hang are short, you can add a lower rail to double the space available or fit shelves there. If you have the option, choose plenty of shallow drawers rather than a few deep ones, so that you can easily find what you are looking for. See-through Perspex (Plexiglass) or wire is excellent for the same reason.

You might take the concept of built-in furniture one step further and design a walk-in dressing room, either using existing space in the bedroom or space from another room. Industrial racks, rails and shelves might be the answer here as you can afford to make utility the priority, rather than aesthetics.

For many people, nothing beats the old-fashioned look of free-standing bedroom furniture. If you're starting from scratch, look for pieces that offer a good combination of both hanging and folding space. And buy the biggest that the room can accommodate – you can never have too much storage space. Antique linen presses with hanging room are the perfect solution if you can afford only one piece of really wonderful furniture; these often come with deep drawers underneath.

Opposite If you can't afford built-in furniture, you might look for other ways of screening your personal possessions. Here, sandblasted glass panels create a movable, translucent barrier between furniture (also on castors) and possessions. Priority has been given to rails, open shelves and boxes, rather than an expensive exterior.

Above Make the most of what you have: a simple clothes rail is the only essential for hanging clothes. The innovative use of this ladder for folding clothes makes it clear that ingenuity counts for more than a big budget. An old trunk provides more storage.

TIPS

- Feel good about throwing things away. Donate old clothes to charities or sell them.

- Be disciplined. When washed clothes are dry, fold them up and put them away immediately.

- In a busy household, invest in a three-part laundry bin for white, dark and coloured clothes.

- Make getting dressed easier by assembling a collection of co-ordinated garments. Plan your wardrobe the night before; when you come home, change into casual clothes and put your smart outfit out to air before replacing it in your closet. This cuts down on dry cleaning.

- If you keep shoes, hats or winter sweaters in boxes, label them clearly.

- If you're storing things away long-term and are worried about damp, use silica crystals to absorb moisture.

- Store fine fabrics such as chiffons, silks and velvets in separate see-through boxes to protect them.

- Get rid of plastic storage bags. They protect against dust, but the chemicals can damage fine fabrics.

- Choose hangers according to what you are hanging: silk, for example, should be hung on padded satin. Hang belts separately, as they can damage the shape of a garment.

- In a room that doubles as a guest room, you might not want permanent furniture. A collapsible canvas wardrobe stores flat when not in use.

- For natural protection against moths, try cedar products.

Far left A walk-in dressing room such as this one is for many people the height of convenience and luxury. There's something satisfying in such orderly arrangements of jackets, shoes and shirts — everything has its rightful home and is maintained to the highest standards.

Left and above In this chic apartment, Japanese-style sliding doors have been used to conceal well-organized cupboard interiors, creating a clean Zen-like space. Inside, stepped drawers create extra hanging space and more surfaces, while open shelves make the perfect place for folded clothes.

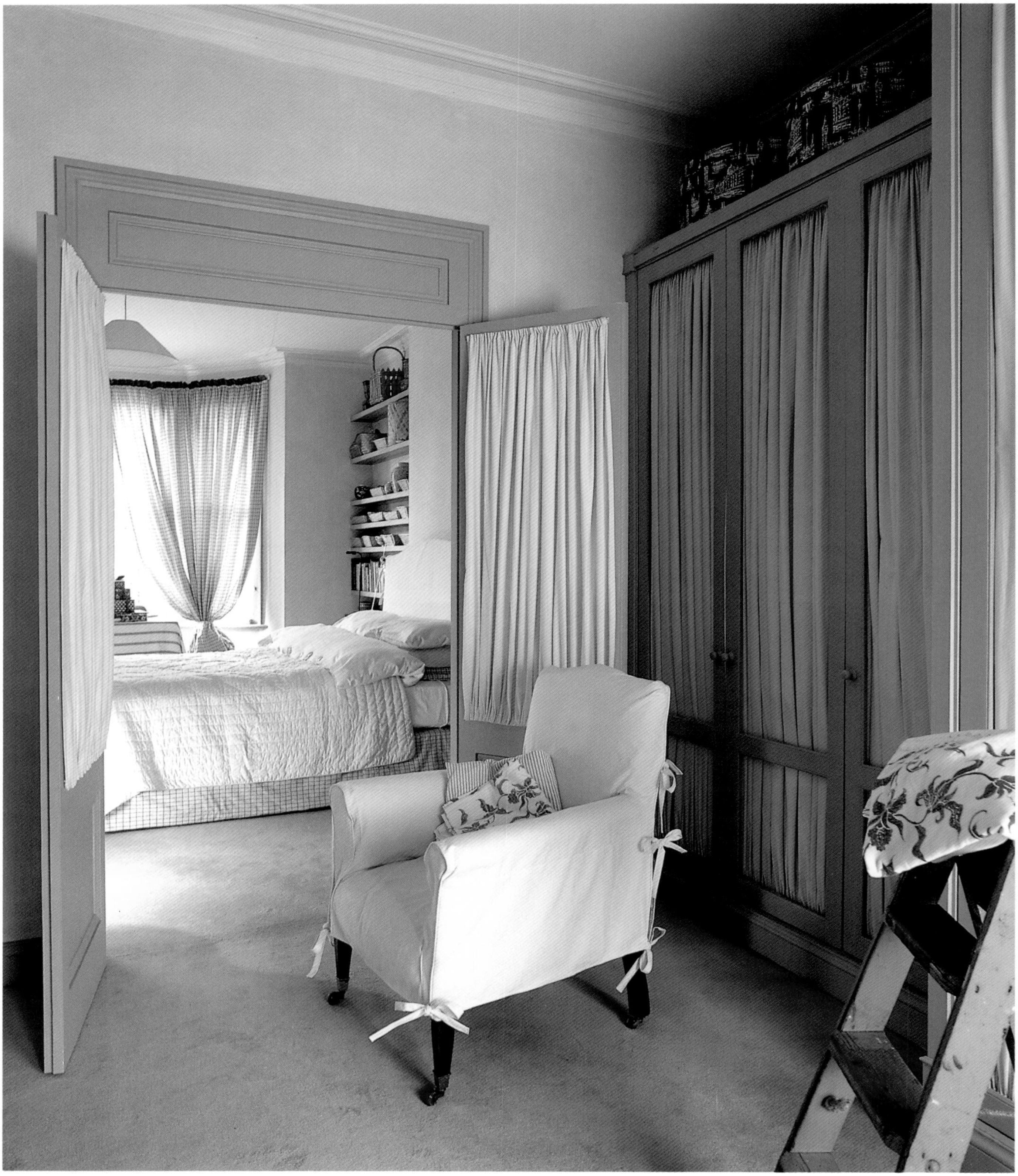

Organizing your wardrobe is not just about having enough hanging and folding space: it's about facing up to what you really wear and what you don't, and getting rid of all the excess clutter in your closets. If you have ever wailed that you don't know what to wear, as you hunted through endless combinations of shirts, trousers and jackets, then the time has come for some selective culling.

Set aside some time to take a long, hard look at your clothes. You are going to make a pile of clothes to take to your local charity shop. Feel good about this – someone, somewhere needs these clothes more than you do. The first thing to go on the pile is anything you haven't worn in the last two years, whether it's because of the fit, the fashion, or simply the fact that you never liked it as much when you got home as you did in the shop. Repeat this process with shoes, belts, hats and gloves. Discard ancient underwear and anything with a stain on it or anything with a repair that you know you will never get around to mending. Now pack the decent rejects into heavy-duty plastic bags and deliver them on the same day to that charity shop – it has all been a waste of time if you push the whole lot under the bed.

Take a look at what is left. Make a new pile, this time of anything that can be put into long-term high-level storage – whether in the attic or at the top of a cupboard. This might include out-of-season clothes and coats; sports equipment that is rarely used, such as skiing or diving gear; and things of sentimental value like your

first ball gown or wedding dress. These should be wrapped, boxed and labelled.

What remains in your wardrobe is what you actually wear. You now know not only what you have, but also what you do not have. This should make shopping a more rewarding experience. Separate the short hanging clothes from the long hanging ones and then divide them according to colour. The space you have created under the short hanging section is ideal for boxes of shoes and other accessories.

Opposite *A feminine dressing room leads off a boudoir-style bedroom; pleated silk panels reflect the romantic mood and protect clothes from dust.*
Above left *If you have several pairs of shoes, it helps to label the boxes. Photos tacked on the outside will help you locate the required pair easily.*
Left *If you prefer to display your wares, these canvas shoe caddies are the perfect home for casual shoes. They can be bought free-standing or hung from the back of a door.*
Above *The interior of this gentleman's wardrobe is divided into hanging, folding and shoe space.*

We spend a huge amount on our clothes and shoes, yet if we don't look after them properly our money is wasted. It stands to reason that it's worth maintaining them properly. Deal with stains and repairs immediately — there's nothing more frustrating than taking your chosen outfit out of the closet only to find you can't wear it. Remove plastic covers from the dry cleaning as soon as you can and leave the garment to air before putting it away. Choose the best hangers you can afford for your clothes — cedar is the blue chip of the hanger world because the scent repels moths. If you're paying a week's wages for one outfit, it makes sense to buy a decent hanger for it at the same time. If you're very short of hanging space, look for hangers that are designed to take five or six garments at a time.

When putting clothes into long-term storage, make sure they're wrapped properly — protective cotton holders are better than plastic because they allow fabrics to breathe. Make sure whites are stored away from harsh sunlight as it makes them yellow. Pack with tissue paper to minimize creasing, and give each garment its own box where possible.

Look after shoes too. They are often the first thing people look at and they say a lot about you. Make sure you keep them well heeled and clean. You don't have to buy shoe trees — stuffing them with paper is just as effective. The space under the short hanging clothes is perfect for shoes — you can buy special cubby-holes that stack up underneath so that each pair is protected. This is also the perfect solution if you are short of folding space, as sweaters and shirts can be stored in this way too. When you buy a hat, make sure you also buy a hat box — not only is it functional, but it looks attractive.

There is a multitude of purpose-built holders for storing clothes: special hangers for ties and belts; and custom-made dividers that separate socks into pairs or keep your underwear in order.

Far left *Find containers that suit the scale of the items you want to organize – these wire dishes are perfect for costume jewellery.*

Left *Save time – if you have a fondness for a particular item and own several types, store them in such a way that you can find the one you want easily. Hooks for watches are the ideal solution.*

Below *Store like with like – ties should be sorted by colour or pattern, or kept with co-ordinating shirts.*

Below right *Choose hangers carefully – they should be strong enough to support the garment well.*

Bottom right *Belts should be hung or rolled.*

TIPS

- Graduate your hanging clothes by size – all your short clothing at one end and long at the other, and then arrange by colour. That way, you will not only know what you own, but will also free up space under your short hanging clothing for storing shoes, handbags and the like.
- If you travel frequently and often come home with a pocketful of foreign coins, store them in a set of jars with the country labelled on the front.
- If you keep things in boxes, whether shoes, hats or winter sweaters, then you must label them correctly. If you have a lot of one particular item, then take this a step further – either take a photograph or draw a simple sketch of the contents and stick it on the outside of the box.

Once your clothes are in order, take a look at the rest of the room. Do you need so much clutter on the bedside tables and the dressing table? Give yourself another chunk of time to sit down and sort through what you have. Remember, the secret is to store like with like. If one of your greatest pleasures is to read in bed, then make sure you have some bookshelves nearby. If you have one drawer where a motley collection of outcasts gather – safety pins, loose change, old tickets, business cards – then divide them up into their relevant groups and store them in separate containers. You will probably find that you can throw away half of them anyway. If your make-up is a sprawling mess, then follow the same principles as you did with your wardrobe but this time throw away anything that is more than six months old – it's unhygienic to keep using it. And don't throw all your valuables into one container – apart from being a boon for thieves, you will never be able to find a pair of matching earrings or cufflinks. Separate costume jewellery from the good stuff (find a secure place for the latter), and then divide it into categories. You don't have to buy one of the commercially available jewellery holders – make use of fishing tackle boxes, tool kits and cutlery drawers. You can hang long beads and necklaces on the sort of hanger bought for ties.

If your bedroom has multiple functions, but you want to keep it looking like a bedroom, try to find ways of hiding pieces of equipment that don't blend in. Conceal

a computer desk behind a screen; ditto a multi-gym or filing cabinet. This screen might be free-standing and purpose-made, but it could just as easily be draped fabric or a tall piece of furniture. Make sure you have enough shelf and drawer space for all the extra paraphernalia. Bulky items such as weights, suitcases or ski boots are best kept out of sight, but you might want to make a focal point of a musical instrument. Just make sure you find an accessible place to store the sheet music.

Above This cowhide bedspread is the height of kitsch and the bed is arranged so that it takes centre stage. However, attention has also been given to sensible storage: clothes rails hung at two heights line one wall and there are free-standing pieces of furniture for smaller items. The table on castors is a fun design, but is also very functional. The whole constitutes a clever use of available space.
Right Weather-beaten, old-fashioned pieces of luggage look wonderful and make an interesting alternative to conventional drawers. They also have the advantage of being fully portable.

Left *This mannequin's hand is perfect for hanging costume jewellery on – look around junk shops and charity shops for other unusual finds. Displaying your wares makes it so much easier to find the ones you want to wear.*

Below *If you don't own a conventional dressing table, mock one up with available pieces of furniture. Here, a generous-sized mirror is propped up on a disused dining table. The wicker trunk provides storage space and an extra surface, while a charming display of baskets, bowls and cake stands makes an attractive home for personal treasures.*

GUEST ROOMS

There's nothing worse than staying with friends or family and finding their possessions crammed into every available drawer, closet and shelf. Guest rooms often end up taking the overflow from the rest of the house because you can shut the door and not look inside too often, but they should be welcoming as well and that means providing adequate storage.

Start by taking a long hard look at what you use your guest room for. Repeat the process you went through in the bedroom, discarding anything that is no longer used. Can any of the rest be packed away long-term? Perhaps you need to install a high shelf on which boxes can be stored. How much storage your guests need depends on how long they will be staying, and what manner of things they are likely to bring with them. Apart from clothes and shoes, for which they need a suitable amount of hanging, folding and stacking space, will there be enough room for luggage, golf clubs, travel cot (crib) or photographs? Is there a mirror handy for drying their hair or cleansing their face, and are the power points situated in the right place? Is there a suitable bedside light for reading in bed, and is the bed aired and comfortable?

If you have a long-term guest, such as an au pair, try to make the room as comfortable and functional as possible. It might only be a tiny box room, but you can improve the storage space with very little effort. Increase hanging space by fixing hooks on the back of the door; put up plenty of shelving for personal effects; and

buy stackable cubby-holes for shoes and folded clothes. If you don't want your walls ruined, provide pinboards where letters, postcards and mementoes can be tacked. If the room is very cramped, offer to store bulky items, such as luggage or sports equipment, in other parts of the house. Your au pair will be a lot more happy and helpful if she understands from the beginning that everything in your house has its own home, including her own possessions.

Left *This cozy guest bedroom has everything a visitor could want – a comfortable bed, pretty view and plenty of storage. The washstand is ideal in such a compact space – note how shelves have been positioned at the side so that clean towels and face cloths can be found easily. The overall effect is clean, welcoming and comfortable.*

Above *In this bedroom, the needs of a visiting student are well catered for: a free-standing unit offers space for clothes and a table near the bookcase provides a useful study area. Most of the furniture is on castors, making it extra versatile.*

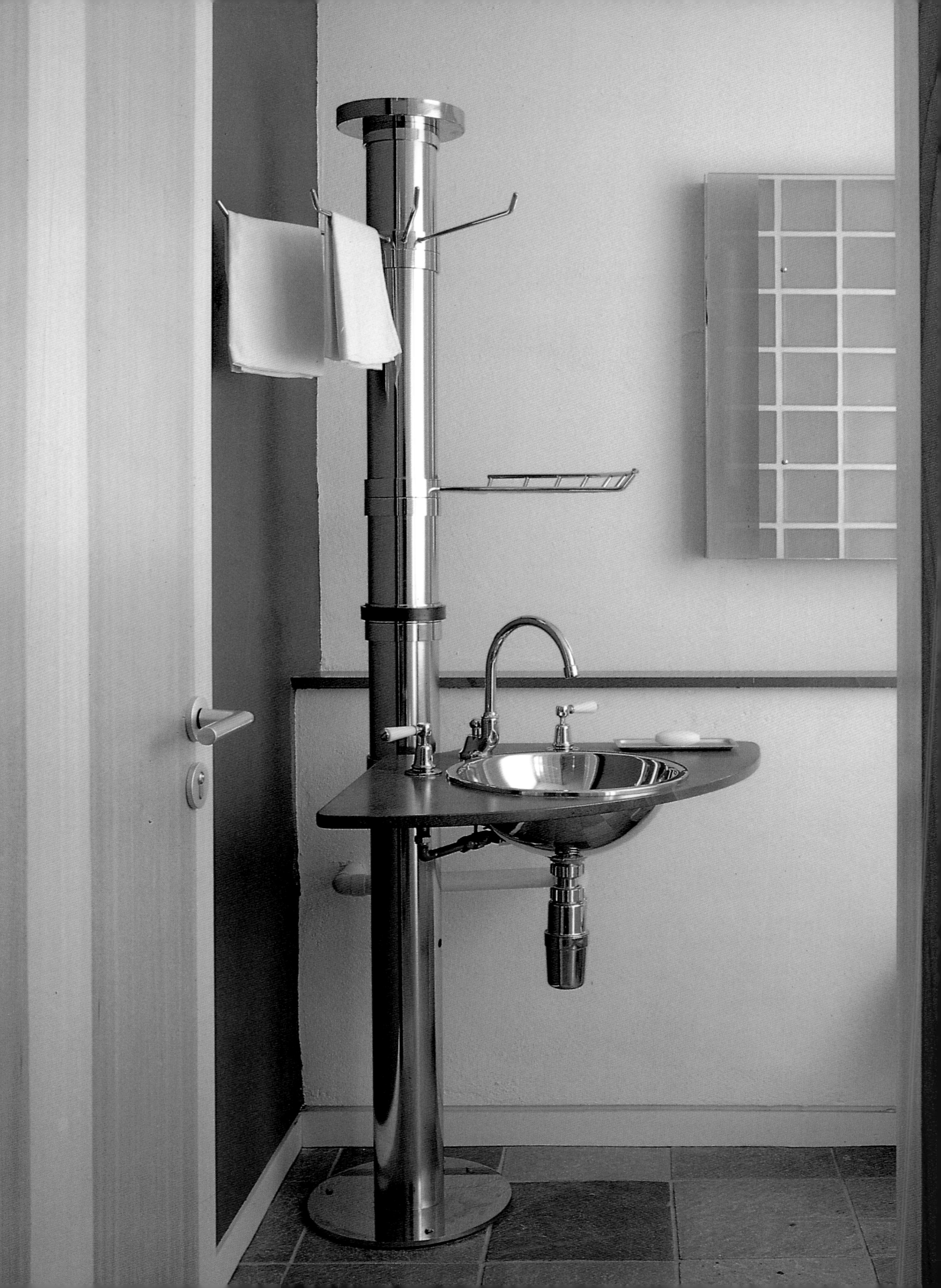

The golden rule when planning the layout of a bathroom is to combine function with comfort. This is a room for unwinding in, pampering yourself, enjoying a refreshing shower or a long, luxurious bath. But it's also the room that is often commandeered for other activities: washing clothes, working out or storing linen. Size may be an obstacle – all too often the bathroom is the smallest room in the house, so every bit of space must be used as efficiently as possible.

Even large bathrooms present problems, as they often look cold and clinical. That is why the bathroom is often an awkward room to design successfully and why it poses so many difficulties when it comes to storing things efficiently. However, these problems are by no means insurmountable. It is simply a question of recognizing that – just as in other key rooms of the house – the bathroom is in fact a series of zones: bathing, shaving, making-up and so on may take place within the same area, but require their own storage solutions. Some of these may be small – a basket for nail-care products; others large – a hamper for towels. It is simply a question of determining what is to be kept where. All sanctuaries require order.

The first thing to do is to work out what you use the bathroom for, who else uses it and how much time they spend there. Make a list of all the things that need to be stored – it might surprise you in its variety. Almost certainly you will have to allow space for towels, toiletries, medicines and toilet paper. But you may also have to allow for dirty laundry, clean linen, beauty appliances, home gym equipment, cleaning products, washing machine, make-up, books, baby bath and changing mat, bulk-bought washing powder and nappies (diapers), bathroom scales and bath toys.

If you're working with an existing bathroom, you might already have come up with some storage solutions, but if you're designing a bathroom from scratch, it's worth thinking about these factors when you draw up your initial plan. As with other areas of the house, make time to draw up a scaled layout of the bathroom, including all its fixtures. Only then will you be able to work out how to use the space most efficiently. If appropriate, take professional advice on the installation of laundry equipment – certain models can be stacked on top of each other to free up floor space – and make sure you provide adequate ventilation.

Before decorating or tiling, consider where you want to position towel rails or fitted shelves. Make use of awkward spaces. Triangular shelves, for example, can be fitted easily into the corners of the bathroom; window sills can double as shelves; and doors can be rehung for extra space. Look for ways of boxing in fixtures

to provide pockets of hidden storage space. If the bath is being fitted from scratch, you might consider setting it into a platform. Not only does this create an interesting focal point, but it also offers an abundance of storage space. You might even consider cutting into the wall to create a recessed niche, or incorporating one into the design of your bath panelling by making it longer than it needs to be.

Where you want a lot of storage, your best option is to install floor-to-ceiling fitted cupboards. If you don't want to make a feature of these, flat panels will give them the appearance of a wall. If you don't have the money for fitted cupboards, look for other ways of providing floor-to-ceiling screening, like blinds or sliding doors. And don't forget 'dead' spaces, such as the backs of doors, the ceiling or the space over the toilet – all these offer potential for storage and yet they're often overlooked in the streamlined bathroom. Even the tiniest of bathrooms can amaze you with its possibilities once you look at it architecturally.

Opposite top *If you don't have much horizontal space, look for ways of utilizing the vertical. Here, a high-level pegboard makes the perfect place for hanging wash bags and towels.*
Opposite bottom *Built-in cupboards are as useful in the bathroom as they are in the bedroom; rolled towels take up less room than folded ones.*
Left *Make the most of architectural features – an alcove is ideal for shelves on which much-loved possessions can be displayed. Perspex (Plexiglass) boxes on the washstand show when supplies are running low; a wicker basket for towels looks natural.*

STORAGE OPTIONS

Whether you choose cupboards, shelves, drawers, hooks or rails, the material they are made from is all important. Bathrooms are hot, steamy places and you want furniture that can withstand a range of temperatures, not to mention condensation. Laminates are the most practical choice, but more attractive options include treated wood, toughened glass, plastic or wicker. Chrome, coated wire and plastic are the most suitable materials for shower and bath accessories. Your choice will depend as much on the aesthetics of the room as its function.

Before you buy new pieces of bathroom furniture, take a close look at what's there already. See whether you could jazz up existing cupboards by painting the doors or covering them with vinyl wallpaper. If the interiors are impractical, why not customize them with commercially available baskets, racks and hooks to make them more efficient? Many of the accessories sold to customize kitchen cupboards can just as easily be applied to the bathroom, such as pull-out metal baskets, towel rails and waste bins.

When choosing furniture or accessories for the bathroom, think about which style of bathroom to go for. Strong unifying colours help to create a feeling of order, but so does keeping to a particular style. In a bathroom with a neutral colour scheme, you might choose pull-down rattan blinds and lots of baskets, but in a contemporary one you could go for flat, featureless cupboards and uniform chrome containers. If you like frills and

flounces, then hide what you can behind fabric skirts and pretty screens; and if you favour a period look, make a feature of antique bottles, pots and jars.

Some packaging is a design feature in its own right, so why not display it on open shelving in a prominent position? Remember that creating a unified look is not just a matter of aesthetics, it's about spending time cleaning knick-knacks, dusting perfume bottles and keeping the bathroom in order.

Left *Free-standing furniture gives a bathroom a homely, comfortable feel. The deep drawers of this pine chest also offer plenty of storage space.*

Below left *An old filing cabinet has been renovated and painted to make a practical alternative to the usual bathroom cabinet. Deep drawers are essential for towels and linen, and each can be labelled with the contents.*

Below *Of course, you can follow the minimalist approach and allow nothing in your bathroom but the bath itself. Here, a low wooden panel is the only division between bathroom and bedroom.*

TIPS

- Get rid of out-of-date cosmetics and medicines – you need the space, and it is dangerous and unhygienic to keep them for too long.
- Keep towels where they will stay dry and aired, on a warm towel rail or on shelves above the hot-water cylinder.
- Don't keep shampoo or shower gel on the floor of the shower as it might pick up mould.

- Keep miniature sizes of your personal-care products in travel-size containers.
- Don't allow old magazines and newspapers to pile up in the bathroom.
- Keep spare toilet paper close by, particularly in a guest bathroom.
- Keep a checklist of first-aid essentials on the back of the medicine cabinet door, and check regularly to see if supplies are running low.

Below A surface is useful — but a surface crammed with containers of all shapes and sizes is ten times so. Here, bathroom goodies have been sorted into related groups and placed in containers that suit their scale. Flower pots, for example, are the perfect place for collections of brushes and loofahs. Only items that are attractive in their own right are on display — the rest are kept out of sight in the painted washstand. Remember that you don't have to spend a fortune buying commercial bathroom holders — take a tip from this and look for new ways of using things you already own.

Above The golden rule of bathroom planning is never to let the toilet paper supplies run out. This is a witty way of ensuring just that — by displaying them in wire school shoe baskets, the owners of this Victorian house have made them a feature of the room and devised a way of spotting instantly when they need to be replenished.

Right Some containers are so attractive in their own right that it seems a shame to cram them with goods. These rustic wicker baskets suit the simplicity of a tongue-and-groove panelled bathroom and can be lifted down when needed.

Once you have chosen your furniture, you then need containers of every size and shape for more specific items. That way you can utilize every corner of available space, without creating a horrible muddle in each drawer and cupboard.

As with other areas of the house, the first step is to pare down your possessions. The time has come to throw away dusty bars of soap, forgotten half-empty bottles of shampoo, ancient medicines (return these to your doctor for disposal), decrepit toothbrushes and any object that has found its way into the bathroom by chance rather than by design. Think of the bathroom as a series of zones, rather than as one space, when planning where to put things: there might be a zone for shaving, for make-up, for sorting laundry, for pedicures, for massage oils and so on. Each zone needs an individual storage solution. As always, the key to successful storage is to keep like with like.

Boxes, baskets, jars and bottles all provide attractive possibilities for storing particular items, but don't limit yourself to choosing from existing ranges of bathroom accessories: borrow ideas from elsewhere in the house – kitchen storage jars, for example, come in lots of different styles and in a wide range of sizes.

There are custom-made holders now for make-up and make-up brushes, contact lens equipment, nail-care products and cotton balls. But you don't have to be so restricted – wicker baskets can be used for everything from magazines and towels to toilet paper rolls and unopened soap, while nylon string bags are the perfect home for children's bath toys. Think about customizing containers intended for other purposes – cigar cases, pencil holders, wine racks and hat boxes all offer possibilities. The only rule you need apply is that the scale of the thing to be stored matches the scale of the container it is to be stored in.

If you are desperate to save surface space, then buy shampoos and shower gels that can be hung from a shower head. Suction-pad bathroom accessories are ideal in a rented home where you can't fix permanent shelves or hooks. Be creative when assessing your space – a ceiling-hung rack with pulley, like those seen in kitchens, is ideal for over the bath, while endless things can be stored on the back of the bathroom door – not only the obvious bathrobe, but also custom-made cubby-holes for slippers, hangers that hold multiple garments and holdalls with pockets for safety pins and hair bands.

EXTRA STORAGE

Subject your towels, sheets and pillow cases to the same ruthless treatment that you have applied elsewhere in the house – discard those that are grey, tattered, washed rough, or simply too ugly to contemplate using again. Now you only need to find enough space for the ones you use and like. Decide how many of these should be hidden away and how many displayed. Clean towels should always be on display as it's embarrassing for guests to find themselves without one. However, don't stack them in a single vertical tower that will fall over when they take one; divide them into two or three manageable stacks on narrowly spaced shelves.

Linens should be cleaned thoroughly before being stored away, and ideally should be placed in a dark, well-aired section of the room. If condensation in the bathroom prevents you storing towels or linen where you want, try fitting cupboard doors more tightly or adding waterproof liners. Good ventilation should guard against the build-up of condensation.

Make sure towels are dry and well aired before you put them away – there's nothing worse than pulling one out only to find that it's got that sickening, musty smell. Heated towel rails are a boon because of this. Don't bother with chemical air fresheners in cupboards, but try natural ones instead, such as bags of pot-pourri or scented herbs. Remember, the bathroom is a sanctuary for the senses so indulge at your leisure.

If your bathroom is also your laundry room, you will need a container for dirty

Above Towels should be clean, dry and accessible – this bamboo frame makes an attractive alternative to a conventional towel rail.

Right Towel rails are hung at different heights and baskets fixed to the wall to exploit blank wall space.

Opposite top There is something luxurious about plump white folded towels – here, they are displayed on open shelves, making them an integral part of this streamlined modern bathroom.

Opposite bottom The chrome towel rail curves around the basin unit to accentuate its shape and provide optimum hanging space.

linen, but don't limit yourself to the conventional wicker laundry basket. Consider investing in one with separate sections for whites, darks and coloureds – it will save you lots of time when you come to sort the washing.

You should always have a supply of cleaning products handy in the bathroom. If there are no children in the house, you could conceal these behind a door or fabric skirt under the basin. But if safety is an issue, you should put them at as high a level as possible. The space over the toilet is often ignored, yet it offers enormous potential in a very small bathroom for items such as these. You could either fit shelves yourself, or have a look at some of the commercially available cabinets that are designed with this space in mind.

Medicines also raise safety questions in a family home. Again, store them at a high level, and make sure that child-proof lids are firmly in place. Never store tablets or other medicines in containers that might look attractive to young children or deceive elderly people. Also make sure you clear out the cupboard regularly – at least every six months.

If you store large bulky items like ironing boards or baby baths in the bathroom, try to keep them out of sight – place them in cupboards or exploit the space created where pipes are boxed in. Failing that, take a tip from the Shakers and fix pegboards around the upper wall. That way you can simply hang the offending objects out of the way – they might not be out of sight, but the overall effect can be an interesting one.

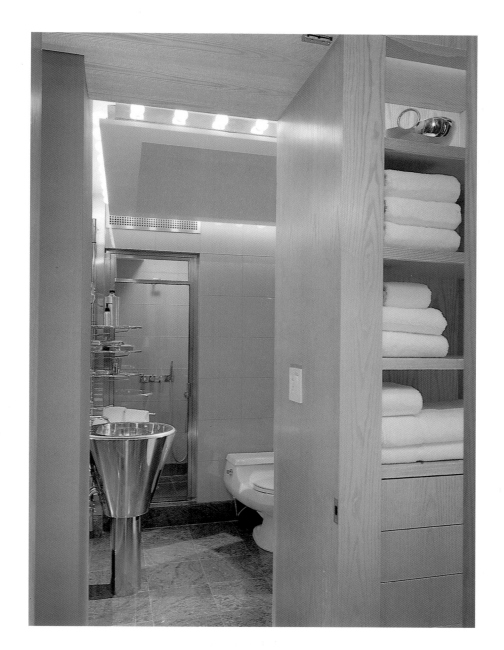

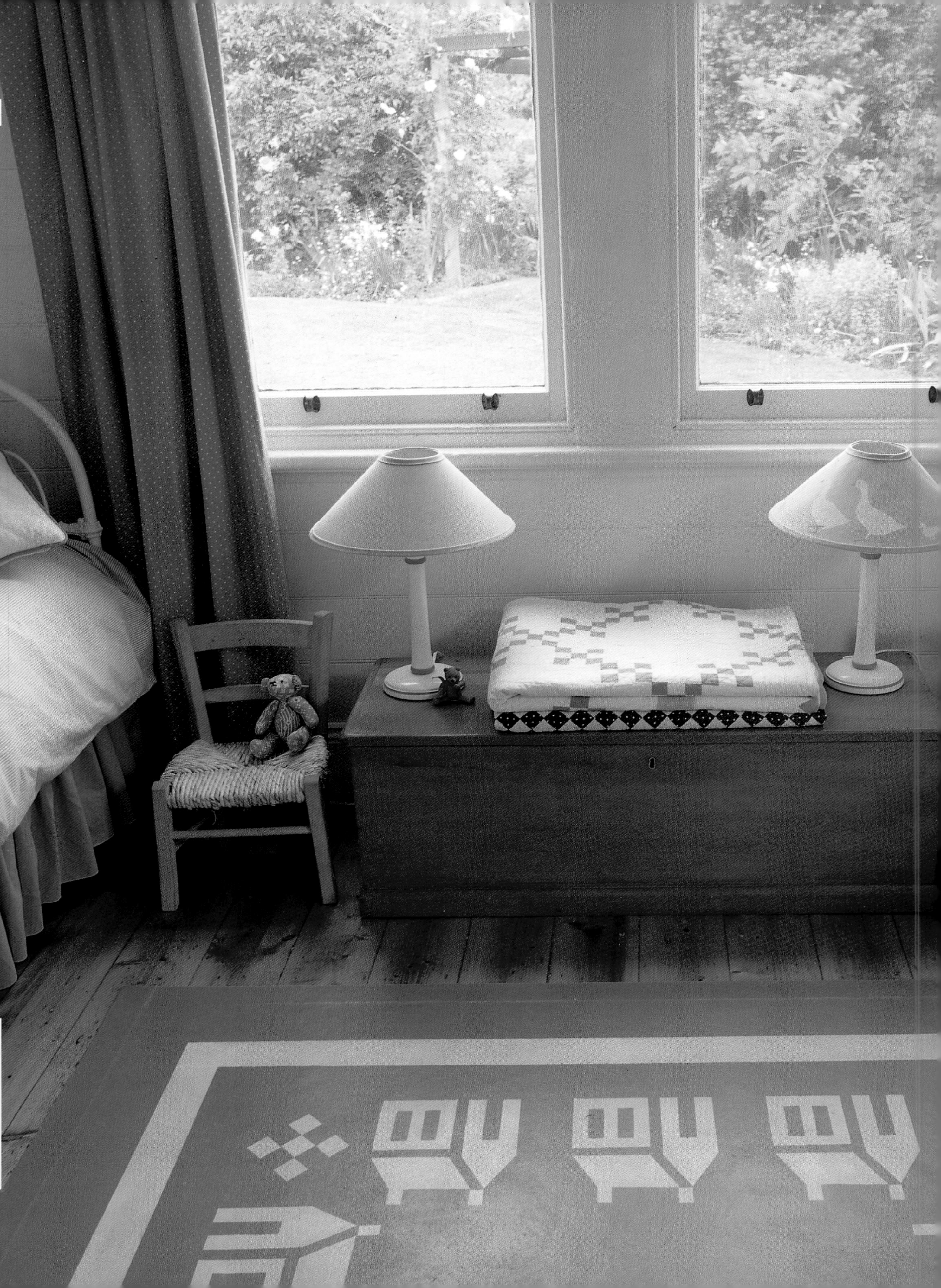

CHILDREN'S ROOMS

The challenge of decorating a child's room is in making him or her feel good about being there. Very young children need security and stimulation. Older children need a combination of coziness and excitement. Teenagers want privacy from the family and a place to be with friends. What this calls for, of course, is flexibility, both in the layout of a room and in the furniture you install. Storage needs will change as children get older, both in terms of what will need storing and how accessible it must be. So make it easy for both them and you – deal with the present, but look to the future. It is a fallacy that children like to live in mess – too often they are simply not provided with enough suitable storage options. In many ways, children's rooms are an example of one-room living at its most difficult: one person's clothes, activities and precious possessions all crammed into a too-small space. Shelves that are too high, drawers that stick and huge toy boxes in which everything is a muddle all conspire to keep the child fighting a state of chaos. Even teenagers don't necessarily mean to live in a tip – but is there really ample space for their increasing number of possessions? Give them a hand – show them how it's done.

ASSESSING SPACE

First tackle the fundamental questions. How many bedrooms do you have? What size are they? How many children do you have? Are you planning to have any more? Is there a playroom? If not, where is most of the playing to be done – in the bedroom or in the living room? Tempting as it might be to ban toys from the general living area, you do have to consider safety: some children simply aren't old enough to be left to their own devices. Nor do they want to be.

Let us say a home has three bedrooms. The usual option is to use the largest one, the master bedroom, for the parents; the second bedroom for the older child; and the smaller bedroom, often no bigger than a box room, for the youngest. But is this the logical solution? It might be better for the parents to use the second bedroom and for the children to share the largest one – so freeing the third room for an office or guest room. If children are going to share a room, think about ways of

giving them some privacy within it: freestanding shelving units or screens, for example, can be used to create a partition down the middle.

Consider location too: the smaller the child, the nearer to you he or she has to be. Don't assume that your teenage son will want the second biggest bedroom. He might well prefer the box room in the attic where he is guaranteed some privacy.

When assessing the space you have, don't just think of the immediate future. Consider how your child's needs are going to change as time progresses; flexibility is the key word. This is when modular systems of furniture really come into their own, providing as they do desks, spare beds, private cubby-holes and under-bed storage, all of which can be changed around as a child gets older. Never buy child-sized furniture, no matter how adorable it looks in the shop: children grow bigger, so buy big.

A baby takes up very little space – the clothes are small and he or she hasn't yet had a chance to collect numerous toys. In fact, yours might start off by sleeping in your own bedroom. But there's a lot of baby paraphernalia that does take up space: travel cot (crib), baby bath, bulk-bought nappies (diapers), baby walker, giant teddies and the like. You might not need much in the way of folding or hanging space, but you do need high-level storage so that you can keep a lot of this out of sight.

Storage for very young children needs to be adult-orientated, to make changing, feeding, bathing and dressing the baby as easy as possible, so, for example, wherever your baby's changing mat is, make sure that there's a shelf nearby for all the necessary creams, cotton balls and powders. You can, of course, buy a complete baby changing unit, which provides pockets for storing every conceivable baby accessory, but remember that your child will outgrow it surprisingly quickly.

As a baby becomes a toddler, low-level storage for toys, games and books becomes more important if you are to encourage your child to undertake some of the tidying. Remember that to a small child a room at night is full of fearful shadows: each piece of junk left on the floor can become monstrous; half-open doors almost certainly mean a witch is lurking in the cupboard; and the space under the bed is an open invitation to child-eating bogeymen! What you need is a well-designed room where everything has a home and where only the clean lines of something familiar and recognizable can be seen.

Of course, the look of the room is important too. It's a place for playing, but also for learning, so you need to make it a stimulating environment. Keep colour schemes and patterns simple and strong – whimsical themes are all very well, but a strong unifying colour helps to create a feeling of order. Safety is paramount as your child begins to grow more independent: don't put things high out of reach, so encouraging him or her to use nearby shelves as a ladder; make sure toy boxes have slam-proof hinges; and don't fix hooks at eye level.

Opposite Built-in furniture is a valuable addition to a child's bedroom, but this need not mean floor to ceiling. Here, a cupboard provides a cubby-hole for toys and games, while the surface above makes an attractive display area. A high-level pegboard can be used to hang things out of reach, but one at a low level is more useful from a child's point of view. *Left* The slide-out tray below this cot (crib) is ideal for storing bulky goods; the manger-style basket above can take all manner of baby paraphernalia. *Below* Surfaces are important – a table to draw at and a window seat that doubles as a work surface.

THE CHILD'S BEDROOM

As children grow bigger, let us say until about the age of ten, they need an awful lot of storage because they acquire a great deal of possessions: shoes for every occasion and activity; clothes for both indoor and outdoor wear; toys, games, puzzles and books; farmyard and railway sets; and eventually computers, music systems and televisions. A space for creative play is obviously needed, but so is somewhere for friends to spend the night – not to mention the ever-expanding collections of computer games and comics. Fortunately, the child is growing in proportion to his or her possessions, so you can make use of both high- and low-level storage. Buy furniture not just for its looks, but for how many things it can contain and its accessibility. Antique pine, for example, looks wonderful, but if the drawers stick, don't be surprised if your child develops an aversion to tidying up.

If your child is very untidy and never clears up his or her room when asked to, take a long hard look at it and ask yourself why. Does he or she have easy access to all the furniture and is it easy to open and to use? Are shelves and rails fixed low enough or is there simply so much on them that nothing can be fitted away easily? Are there enough containers to take all the different types of toys or do they end up being thrown into general holdalls: pencils with playing cards, dice with pieces of jigsaw, cars with soldiers? If so, is it any wonder that whole boxes are emptied in a frantic hunt for the vital ingredient for a certain game?

What is needed is a system. There should be containers for every type of toy: both large and small. As with every room, you should store like with like. Plastic stackable baskets are a boon here: buy them in several sizes and colours and encourage the child to learn a simple code, such as red for Lego, blue for bricks, yellow for cars and so on. As children get older, they love to hoard small fiddly bits and pieces – hair baubles, fake jewellery, cards from cereal packets and foreign coins – so provide a container that

matches the scale of these items. You don't have to buy one specially – egg, cigar and chocolate boxes can all prove very efficient. Once everything in the room has a home, you can start to introduce some ground rules, such as setting a limit on how many types of toys can be played with at any one time. And if the room does become so chaotic that an adult's help is needed, then be constructive about it: offer to tidy the clothes if they tidy the books; then offer to do the Lego if they do

TIPS

- If you can't face throwing away children's clothes and toys of sentimental value, get together with a friend and help each other to have a big clear-out.
- For children who like to collect things, teach them early that quality matters more than quantity.
- Travelling with babies can be traumatic. Keep a checklist and run through it each time you go away.

- Buy plain toy boxes that you and your child can paint and decorate together. This will save you money, and make the child more inclined to use them.
- If you're desperate to instil some order into teenage lives, try to find storage options that will appeal to their interests – a state-of-the-art CD rack, a holder for motorbike tools or a really professional make-up organizer.

the bricks. In this way, the children will learn that the secret of tidying is to keep like with like; and that to get a big task done, you often need to carry out a series of smaller jobs.

If the living room becomes a playroom during the day, it may be worth investing in a mobile storage unit so that toys can be tidied away in the evening and pushed out of sight when the grown-ups come out to play. A trolley (cart) on castors is ideal for this purpose and won't cost the earth.

Above As a child grows, his or her possessions begin to multiply. If you don't want to be faced with chaos, you must provide enough storage – not just furniture, but containers too. This cheerful room has a generous-sized toy box and plenty of plastic tidy-alls for toys.

Top right Make storage fun by customizing pieces of furniture – yellow-and-white gingham gives a new lease of life to a rather utilitarian chest-of-drawers.

Right Blinds are an excellent way of hiding toys when not in use – this stars and stripes design is both functional and fun.

THE TEENAGER'S ROOM

Of course as children become teenagers, their needs change again. Few want to be reminded of childhood – it's a bit too close for comfort – so don't be surprised if they want to see the back of that modular set of furniture, no matter how practical it might be. They want a more adult look to their room: think one-room living rather than a bedroom. This has to be a living room, with space for entertaining, working, relaxing and sleeping – not to mention making as much noise as possible. Display is still important, so don't gripe about the damage to the walls – it might be the perfect place for a collection of beer mats or rock concert tickets.

You might not be able to impose tidiness on teenagers, but you can ensure they have enough space to store possessions should they want to. Clothes are an obsession at this age, so provide as much wardrobe space as possible. This doesn't have to mean separate pieces of furniture – a rail on wheels as found in clothing shops, plus a couple of wardrobe tidies with compartments for shoes and folded sweaters, might prove just as popular. Bunk beds might get the thumb's down, but a high-level platform bed with space underneath for a desk or sofa could be acceptable. If you don't want to splash out on a conventional sofa, a futon makes an inexpensive seat as well as a spare bed for overnight guests. Shelves of different depths and heights – preferably fully adjustable ones – are a must for growing collections of CDs, computer games and videos. A study space is also essential – at

its most basic, this will consist of a table, drawers and shelves in a well-lit corner of the room, but to the teenager it's style that counts – industrial shelving might get the thumbs up where fake teak would not. Canvas boxes can store assorted papers and a pinboard on which reminders and deadlines can be posted should prompt a professional approach to studying.

When it comes to personal effects, the same rules apply here as in the rest of the house: store like with like. Wicker baskets

of different colours can separate cleansers from moisturizers, cotton balls from nail care, razors from hair gel. If there's a basin in the bedroom, provide shelves, drawers and containers for make-up, shaving gear, shampoo and soap. Once one set of things is efficiently stowed away, your child will hopefully find it tempting to follow suit in the rest of the room. If none of this makes any difference, then there's only one thing for it: keep the door closed at all times and simply don't look in!

Far left Furniture has been chosen for its flexibility – chairs roll out into futons for friends spending the night, while pillows and a throw transform the bed into a generous sofa.

Left Make sure your teenager has enough surfaces handy – a simple bedside table like this one is doubly useful when a container is added.

Below left Not every teenager wants the hi-tech look – some like to be surrounded by familiar pieces of furniture that they have known and loved from childhood. The fireplace in this cozy bedroom has been removed to make room for built-in book shelves, and the mantelpiece is a display surface for remnants of the recent past. Don't forget how important wall space is for teenagers – not just for posters, but for pinboards of personal mementos, calendars of events and postcards from friends.

Above Most teenagers would be happy to spend time in this attractive bed-sit. Bright fabrics, bold paint colours and comfortable seating make it a relaxing sanctuary away from prying parents.

WORKSPACES

The number of people working from home is rising dramatically year by year. Some have negotiated this with their employers; some are self-employed; others are pursuing interests that they hope will offer them employment in the future. Even in households where people are employed full-time elsewhere, you will often find a computer, fax and phone in a corner of a bedroom. But home offices are not the only symptom of social change – there is a rash of studios and workshops also appearing, as people adapt to losing jobs and creating others. The work-space is now as integral to our homes as the kitchen and bathroom. All of this calls for a rethink of how we allocate space within our homes.

A dedicated work room is superior to a work area within another room in many ways: no need to clear everything out of sight at the end of the day; somewhere private to make and take calls; an atmos-phere of purposeful and ordered calm.

It is now clearer than ever that people increasingly expect satisfaction from their work as well as material gain, and that often goes hand in hand with the quality of life that working from home can bring. So view the work room not as a loss of space, but as a change to welcome.

Above *A home office needn't take up a lot of space – this high-level balcony is tucked away from busier corners of the apartment, but is the perfect size for table, chair and low storage unit.*

Opposite *When assessing your own space, pay attention to the vertical as well as the horizontal. This architect-designed mews house represents compact living at its best. The desk is designed to fit over the door frame and the chair is positioned on a narrow ledge where it's at optimum height. A transparent screen cuts down on noise, while integrating the office into the rest of the home.*

For many people, a place in which to work, whether professionally or at a hobby, is paramount in the home. This workplace could be as basic as a table tucked away in a bedroom corner where household accounts can be tackled or Christmas cards designed, or as sophisticated as an entire office equipped with computer, fax machine and printer. Most work areas fall into one of three categories: a home office where paperwork is the priority; a studio devoted to creative pursuits like music, pottery, photography or dance; or a workshop for woodwork, metalwork or mechanical projects. Garages and outbuildings often come into their own for the latter.

The size and location of the chosen space will be determined by the nature of your work; whether you'll be working there all the time or only occasionally; and whether you'll be sharing with anyone else.

Before you start planning the design of the room, consider the basics: is the light sufficient at all times of the day? Do you have enough power points? Can you take any steps to deaden noise levels? Do you require planning permission to change the use of the building? If you're using a room within your house solely for business purposes, you should take advice as to whether this will leave you liable for an extra tax bill, and whether it's acceptable to your mortgage and household insurance companies.

If you're worried that you don't have enough space to carry out the sort of activity you would like, think again. Most people imagine they need far more space than they actually do. If you assess the space vertically, as well as horizontally, you will soon realize just how much potential a small alcove or outside shed offers. First draw up a list of furniture, tools and stationery you will need to fit into your work area, then draw up a plan of the room and juggle around with the layout until you find a solution. Be prepared to make compromises, if necessary, and remember that how and where you store your equipment will make all the difference to your work.

STORAGE OPTIONS

One of the main differences between a workplace that is integrated into the home and one that is separate from it is the overall style and look of the room. A workshop that is housed in the garage can afford to look like a workshop; a bedroom that also serves as a work area cannot. If your home office forms part of the domestic environment, make sure it has some visual sympathy with the rest of the house. Look at the architectural style of the house, the size and shape of the room and any dominant colour schemes. There's a thin line between creating a professional and organized office in the home and imposing a clinical, stark style that is out of keeping with everything else around you.

Choose furniture and fittings that complement their surroundings or adapt existing pieces so that they fit in with the overall scheme – painting a book shelf, for example, so that it ties in with another feature in the room will make all the difference. Filing cabinets don't have to look like filing cabinets and desks don't have to be square and boxy. Try customizing a piece of period furniture, such as a map chest, blanket box or shop display cabinet. For a desktop, ask a local carpenter to cut MDF (medium-density fibreboard) or plywood into your chosen shape, then paint it to match the room.

If you prefer a period look, take inspiration from the traditional study-cum-library. Scan antique shops for deeply padded chairs and leather-topped desks, or build floor-to-ceiling shelves and fill them with books. If your computer doesn't blend in with the period style, then hide it under a blanket or conceal it in an alcove behind a folding screen. Or for a more streamlined look, commission a workstation – complete with closing doors to hide your machine when not in use.

If yours is a more contemporary room, there are plenty of designs to choose from. But steer clear of black, unless it ties in with the rest of the decor, as it can be overbearing. In a huge space, such as a loft or warehouse, industrial-style shelving can look just right.

TIPS

- Update your files every month. Replace current brochures and throw away outdated information.
- How do you classify your work? By project, vendor, category? Set up a filing system that matches this.
- Save the environment by cutting down on hard copies of work. Save on disk and set up a disk file that mirrors the files on your computer.
- Use see-through files for bills and other important documents – if you can see them, you are more likely to deal with them.
- Desk drawers are usually either shallow and wide or very deep. Use drawer dividers to use the space efficiently.
- Some items, such as old accounts, need to be put into storage – box, and always label clearly.

Left *Finding home office space often involves slicing off a piece from another room. Choose a location where you can work relatively undisturbed, and where there is enough storage space to contain paperwork. The free-standing cupboard to the right of this desk provides generous storage and is used for both professional and domestic purposes.*
Above *A comfortable chair which supports the back properly is essential in a home office. Swivel ones are ideal as they make it possible to access a great deal more – such as the storage boxes behind – than a conventional design would.*

WORKSPACES

HOME OFFICES

If you do need a home office, first decide on its location. Ideally, it should be in the quietest part of the house – don't imagine for a moment that it will be a success if you set up camp in the living room where you have one eye on the television and the other on the kids. In a room that serves another purpose – a guest bedroom perhaps – ensure that everything can be cleared away easily after use and stored out of sight. If you're running the sort of business where clients visit you at home, make sure your work space presents a professional front – it should appear to be as separate from the rest of the household as possible.

When assessing your storage needs, begin by drawing up a list of all the things you need to store. This will include both large pieces of equipment, such as computer, printer, fax machine, modem, phone, answering machine and filing cabinet, and smaller items such as pens, floppy disks, calculator, stationery and reference books. If space is tight, choose equipment that is extra compact – there are plenty of fax machines, for example, that also function as phones and answering machines.

Home computers are to blame for a number of posture and back problems, so wise up to the right way of working at one from the word go. A redundant table and old chair are not the answer. Visit an office supplier and choose a chair with a curved back that really supports your spine. It must have an adjustable height, because your feet should always be flat on the floor and your legs flat on the chair. The chair should support you not only when you sit upright to type, but also when you sit back to read. If you do a lot of copy-typing, invest in a paper-holder so that you don't have to bend your head to read; place this at the same height as the screen. Items you use on a regular basis, such as dictionary or dictaphone, should be situated within easy reach of the desk.

Lighting is important too. Adjustable lights are best for desk work, but don't direct the bulb at the screen or it will dazzle your eyes. Position your screen so that your head is held straight, rather than being tilted either forward or back, and make sure your forearms are straight when your hands are resting on the keys. Try to take regular breaks, as you would in a conventional office, and learn some simple stretching techniques to help you unwind at the end of the day.

If you or the person you live with are obsessive about tidiness, then you should design storage that allows you to hide everything out of sight when you have finished your day's work. Built-in furniture will look smarter than a motley collection of old cupboards and cabinets, but include a few display areas too, such as open shelves, pinboards and doorless cupboards. If your home office is also your living room, consider screening your desk from the rest of the room – folding screens are one answer, while pull-down blinds or sliding doors that blank off an office alcove are another.

There are some simple rules that apply in any office situation. Everything must have a recognizable place either on your desk or in the surrounding storage system; and all documents and possessions should be stored with similar items. There is nothing so frustrating as not being able to locate the right document when a client rings. If you want to appear professional, don't let your filing system or storage cabinets ruin your image. If your desk is overflowing with so much paper that you find it difficult to find what you want, ask yourself how much of this paper is really necessary – we live in a technological age where paper should be virtually

redundant. Make back-up copies of documents onto disks and file these instead of paper documents. If you're sharing the computer with someone else, make sure you each have colour-coded boxes so that your floppy disks don't get mixed up.

Deal with mail immediately – respond to it, file it or throw it away. Discard out-of-date material, including old phone books, catalogues and brochures. The less paper you have, the more easily you will be able to find the pieces that really count.

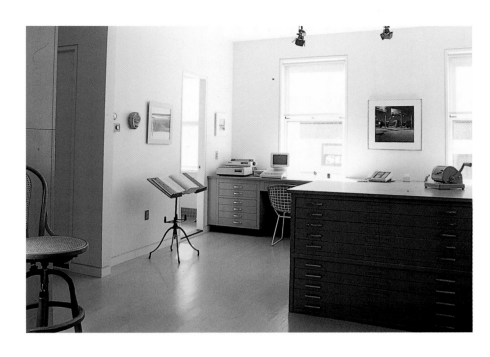

Left This chic library manages to achieve a foot in both camps by looking professional and comfortable. Walls need not be lined with books – these free-standing bookcases are positioned so that both front and back can be used.

Top As working from home becomes the norm for many people, home offices are demanding dedicated space. There has been no attempt to integrate this one into the domestic environment.

Above Professional office furniture can be used successfully in the home office. These pull-out files take up little space and can be catalogued by project.

Above *One of the attractions of a dedicated studio space is that you can keep to the bare essentials – here, a chair, a drawing board, good lighting and a storage trolley (cart) – rather than being over-ridden with domestic clutter.*

Above right *Textile designs are the focus in this studio, so it helps to have piles of them on view for inspiration and reference rather than tucking them away out of sight. Labelled wooden boxes are stacked along one wall, making the most of low-level storage in an attic room. The overall impression is of an energetic and productive workspace.*

If you're intent on pursuing a creative hobby or profession, then studio space of some description is essential. If you're lucky, you might be able to convert a basement, attic or outbuilding, but remember that the success of any room depends not on aesthetics alone, but on how organized it is.

If you need a large sink, for example, make sure there's a work surface of some description close by. Lighting is a prime consideration. Natural light is best for

painting, sculpting and other artistic pursuits, but you can supplement poor light with special fluorescent tubes. If you're planning on making music, look into sound insulation – you might want to seal the walls, ceiling and floors with carpet, cork or other sound-deadening materials.

Whatever your hobby, you will need plenty of storage. Some of this might be permanent, such as built-in shelves or cupboards, but don't overlook portable storage – utility carts, for example, are

perfect for wheeling around tubes of paint, pencils, clay or thread. Toxic materials should be locked away separately.

The best thing about a dedicated space like this is that aesthetics can give way to utility. Go for simple, functional, strong and convenient designs and you will be rewarded with a smooth-running studio. Here you can make use of every available corner – fix racks to the walls and hooks to the ceiling – and exploit all those battered pieces of furniture that are too ugly

to put anywhere else in the house, but still offer excellent storage. Collect plenty of small containers too – jam jars and cigar boxes, wire trays, baskets and flower pots. Decide what should go where and label everything clearly. Remember that you want your storage to facilitate artistic endeavour, not inhibit it, so make sure you put everything away after use. If you keep all like products together and colour-code them, you will have instant access to them whenever you want.

Top A studio can quickly turn into a chaotic mess if a firm hand is not taken. The secret lies in finding a container for every material and piece of equipment. Here, wicker baskets of all shapes make the perfect home for artist's materials. Limiting your choice to one style of container gives a feeling of order.

Above Be inventive when searching for containers – these exotic food cans are the perfect shape and size for collections of pens and pencils. Look in your own store cupboard for boxes, jars and cans that you might be able to put to good use once emptied of their contents.

WORKSHOPS

If the activities you have in mind are heavy-duty like stripping down car engines, making furniture or repairing boats, then a workshop is the answer. A workshop is defined by the machinery it houses, and machinery means noise. So, to keep everyone in the household happy, it is a good idea to keep yours as far away from the main house as possible. There is also likely to be a good deal of dirt, from engine grease to wood shavings, so you need to be able to contain the mess and clean it up on a regular basis. Many garages double as workshops, but some have the disadvantage of leading directly into the house. You need a place to clean up first, so plumb in a sink if necessary and install a row of hooks on which to hang dirty aprons or overalls.

There's no point in starting a job, only to waste 20 minutes hunting for the right tool. Display your tools on racks on the walls and make sure you always put them away after use. Storage areas should be well lit and easily accessible, but they also need to be as dry as possible – tools don't like damp. Maintain them well by cleaning and oiling at regular intervals. Store your tools as near to the main workbench as practical. To avoid accidents, make sure this is well lit so that there's no shadow over your hands while you work.

Some portable storage is also useful, so that you can carry around essential tools. You might want one piece of furniture on castors, such as an industrial-type trolley (cart), or several strong trays or boxes with handles. As well as choosing large pieces of furniture in which to store the essentials, collect small containers too, for nails, screwdrivers, pencils, measures and so on. These should be sorted into like with like, labelled clearly and placed within easy access of your workbench, perhaps on an overhead shelf.

Safety is paramount. Use guards on dangerous equipment; install a fire extinguisher close by; fit an earth-leakage detector to cut off the main electrical supply if a fault develops; and make sure doors are kept locked, so that unaccompanied children never go exploring.

Left Designing a well-ordered workspace doesn't mean hiding everything out of sight – it helps to be able to see the item you are searching for – but it does mean putting things away after use.
Right For people who love what they do – whether professionally or as a hobby – there's nothing quite so satisfying as the sort of display seen here.
Top right In this workshop, every bit of space is used through a combination of hooks, drawers and shelves, so that everything – down to the smallest nut – has its rightful place. Organization like this is truly inspirational.

Tools are expensive and so are worth maintaining well. This is as true in the garden as elsewhere. Keep spades, rakes, trowels and hoes in a dry shed or garage where they won't rust. Don't just fling them down at the end of the day, but spend time scraping off mud and wiping down the metal parts with an oily rag before hanging them up in their allotted place ready for next time.

Garden tools are better hung up high than left on the ground, as this guards against damp and prevents the blades going rusty. Sharp garden knives and seca-teurs (pruning shears) should be placed out of reach of children. If you have your own favourite tools or gloves that you don't want anyone else using, keep them in a separate container and let it be known that it's a capital offence to remove them without permission.

If your gardening efforts are limited to a balcony or roof terrace you will still need somewhere to store a trowel, water-ing can, spare pots and bags of compost. A strong, wall-mounted cupboard is probably the best solution. Make use of limited space with hanging pots and baskets of trailing plants. Window boxes will thrive in a sunny position, but must be fixed firmly to the sill or ledge and kept watered. Maintain house plants with regular feeding and watering, and be on the alert for pests and diseases.

If you have a greenhouse, ensure you get maximum use from it. This means growing plants at two levels, both in the ground and on shelves or benching called staging. Good staging is made from very

strong timber or metal, which supports trays filled with gravel. The moisture evaporating from the gravel maintains the humidity levels in the summer, but beware of excess water in winter as it encourages mildew, which attacks plants.

Staging should be waist high and about 90 cm (3 ft) deep, so that all plants can be reached easily for watering. By growing plants in pots filled with different sorts of composts, you can cultivate a wide variety of plants, whereas in the rest of the garden you are usually hampered by just one type of soil. There's no need to let the area under the staging grow idle either – shade-loving plants such as ferns will thrive here, or use this area to store pots or potting compost. If you need more space, fix narrow shelves above the staging; these should be no more than 15 cm (6 in) wide to prevent them casting too much shadow on the plants beneath.

Hanging baskets can be hooked onto the central support above the greenhouse path. You can grow more than flowers in these – strawberries, herbs and other sun-lovers will do just as well.

Left For the keen gardener, a bench like this is invaluable in the garden. Here, plants can be repotted, seeds pricked out and flowers arranged. A wall-hung cupboard and carefully positioned hooks increase storage potential. The collection of terracotta pots and old-fashioned watering cans is both functional and decorative.

Above The garden is the perfect place for pieces of old furniture that have become too battered for use in the house. Here, old filing cabinets have found a new lease of life as storage drawers for dried herbs and germinating seeds.

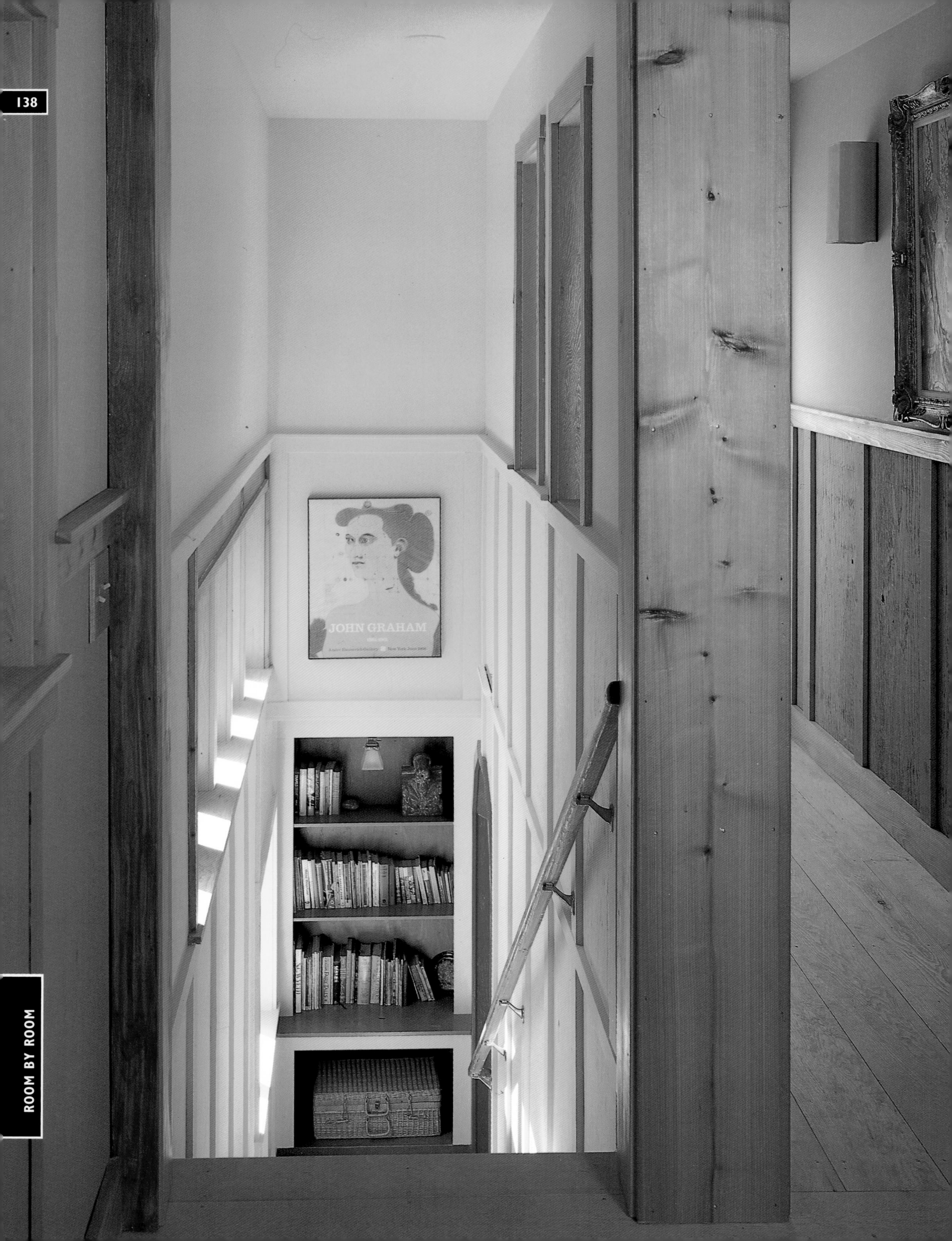
JOHN GRAHAM

Halls and stairs are the traffic routes in a house and so all too often are not considered as proper rooms in their own right. But you need to give them as much thought as you do the rest of your house, especially as they are the first areas seen by guests. So don't let yours let you down – in an ideal world, a well-designed entrance hall should boast durable flooring to withstand the continual tread of wet and muddy shoes; good lighting for both day and night; warm and welcoming colour schemes; and attractive storage for everyone's coats, shoes, keys and bags. But a well-organized hall doesn't stop there. Very often it offers little pockets of space that are not only useful for day-to-day essentials – boots, gloves, umbrellas and so on – but are also valuable for storing away items that don't gravitate towards a natural home of their own: sports gear, old newspapers, sunglasses, keys and the like. That's not to say that you should proudly display such flotsam and jetsam, but if you can utilize a snug corner here and there, it will free up space elsewhere and add to the overall efficiency and comfort of your home. So don't overlook this most fundamental of rooms: a beautifully furnished, well-designed hallway is an asset.

and doesn't turn into a junk depository. Surfaces are important too – a small ledge or a hall table is the ideal home for keys, mail or newspapers.

Unfortunately, because halls are not often considered rooms in their own right, there is a tendency to treat them as second-best and they often become cluttered with unwanted possessions: junk mail, out-of-season coats, chewed-up dog toys, battered slippers. However, they are one of the easiest rooms in the house to regenerate. First clear out all the junk – throw away redundant items and put others, such as out-of-season coats and shoes, into long-term storage elsewhere in the house. Then consider how you will avoid collecting clutter in future. Do you need more pegs for coats, baskets for incoming mail, shelves for telephone directories or racks for shoes? If you have a phone table, make sure there's a jotter and pen nearby where messages can be taken.

If you do buy a piece of furniture for the hall, choose something with lots of storage potential – like a bench with a lift-up seat that can be used to store riding gear or gardening clothes. Consider lighting – is there enough natural light or do you need to boost it with artificial? One of the best ways to focus on special features is with spotlights.

Think about the practicalities of everyday living – where is the best place for muddy boots or wet umbrellas? Perhaps you need a washable rug to protect the floor. If you're hanging up outdoor jackets and raincoats, then move smarter clothes elsewhere – to the bedroom perhaps.

Above *Clean, warm and welcoming – this is how a hallway should look. There are hooks for coats, a bench for bags and a stand for sticks and umbrellas. The message is clear: visitors' needs are catered for and the owners want them to enjoy their stay.*

Opposite *This converted warehouse is designed around the idea of one-space living. The 'hall' is signified by the coat pegs and bike, while an enormous circular bookcase leads into the living area. Storage on this scale is not an option for most home-owners, but look for ways of exploiting alcoves, niches and understairs space to the full.*

magine yourself as a visitor to your own home. Walk through the front door and take a look around. This is the first impression you present to guests – is it a favourable one?

Halls should be welcoming. There should be hooks on which to hang coats and hats; somewhere to leave walking sticks and umbrellas; and a place for outdoor shoes and heavy cases. If you have a built-in cupboard, then make the most of it and make sure it's cleared out regularly

EXTRA STORAGE

Halls are often full of space that has never been fully utilized. If you are desperate for extra storage space to take some of the overflow from elsewhere, then assess what your own hall can offer. Perhaps you have room for low-level, built-in cupboards or one really big piece of furniture like a dresser (hutch) or old-fashioned chest. In a tiny, narrow hall make full use of hooks at both high and low level for hanging everything from coats and dog leashes to hats and shopping baskets.

The space under the stairs might be large enough for a small home office, a writing desk, or a cupboard for storing bikes and other sports equipment. But if there's only enough room for a small storage cupboard, use it for awkward or ugly items that you need on a day-to-day basis, like car tools, craft supplies or bulk-bought household goods. Take a fresh look too at alcoves and other blind spots – can these be converted into places for storing 'extras' like magazines or recyclable jars that haven't found a permanent home elsewhere in the house?

The walls of halls and stairs are perfect display areas where you can create a miniature picture gallery or make displays of items you enjoy collecting, such as mirrors, hats or old comics. Remember that people will brush past these things continually, so store valuable or fragile collections elsewhere and reserve this area for objects that can cope with a little wear and tear. Fix them securely to the wall and don't forget to clean them regularly –

a successful collection must be well displayed and well maintained.

In your quest to unearth new spaces and use them efficiently, don't lose sight of what the hall and stairs are really all about – traffic. People use them to get from one area of the house to the other, so make sure you don't fill them with so much clutter that visitors have to slow down to squeeze past a too-wide hall table, for example, a bicycle or a mountain of overcoats.

Far left Hallways make perfect galleries where pictures and other possessions can be displayed. The home of this sporting enthusiast has been turned into a celebration of angling – even the risers on the stairs are painted with breeds of fish.

Left The hallway is a communal area and is very often where a phone is located – in a busy household, make it the nerve-centre for passing on messages and other information.

Below An avid magazine collector has turned this vertical corridor space into an archive with custom-made units holding catalogued issues.

TIPS

- A plastic tray on the floor is perfect for wet shoes.
- Hang hooks for children's coats low enough for them to reach.
- Divide long hanging coats from short hanging jackets – use the space under the latter for a shoe rack or shelves.
- In a narrow hall, use strong wall hooks and racks to hang bikes, skis, riding hats or surf boards out of the way.

- If you're always losing your keys, invest in a key cabinet to hang in the hall and train yourself to use it.
- You must have one place where anything from heavy school bags to shopping carriers can be dumped temporarily. A low bench or settle is ideal.
- Keep a tray for mail and make sure other members of the family remember to pick up theirs.

PRODUCT

So there you have it. Getting organized and staying that way has never been so easy or so much fun. The chances are that you are now bursting to have a good clear-out and bring order to your home. But if you still need some persuasion, then turn the page for hooks, hangers, holdalls and much more that you just can't be without. But beware: once you start, you just can't stop — buying boxes, bags, baskets and bottles can be addictive, and the choice today is huge. So go on, get a taste of the products available and take the plunge to organize your life.

DIRECTORY

HANGING

1

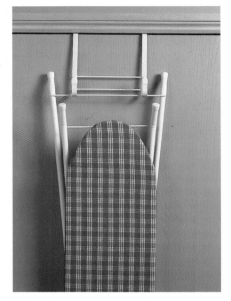

2

3

4

1 HANG 'EM HIGH

Ceiling racks keep pots and pans out of the cupboard and on display.

2 IRONING BOARD CADDIE

The ironing board is a difficult item to store in small spaces – this caddie enables you to utilize wasted door space.

3 SIX-HOOK RACK

Over-the-door hooks take the burden from crowded floor or closet space.

5

4 HANGING BASKETS

Often used to store and ripen vegetables in the kitchen, these are a design feature which can add a splash of colour.

5 MULTIPLE TROUSER HANGER

Save up to 10 cm (4 in) of space in your closet with multiple trouser or skirt hangers – ideal for small closets.

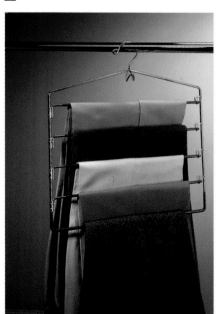

6 SEE-THROUGH STORAGE

Protect your clothing and shoes from dust with see-through plastic storage.

7 PORTABLE WARDROBES

Collapsible wardrobes are great for out-of-season or guest storage. Many are available with castors to make them even easier to roll out when needed.

7

6

8

8 HANGING SHELVES

Sturdy hanging shelves made from cotton canvas attach with Velcro and provide additional shelf space for folded clothing, accessories or shoes.

9 MULTIPLE BLOUSE HANGER

A great space-saving tool, which can hang up to six blouses or shirts in the space of a single hanger.

9

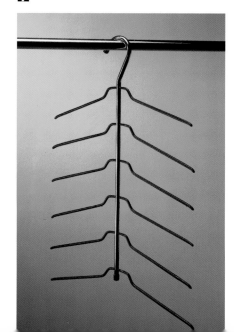

1

1 DESK TIDY

Keep all your notes easily accessible in a rattan organizer. Baskets can be used throughout the house to add a warm accent and are ideal for many storage needs.

2 DIVIDE AND CONQUER

These wire-mesh drawer dividers are the best example of keeping like objects together. They can be used to store kitchen gadgets, costume jewellery or make-up.

2

4

5

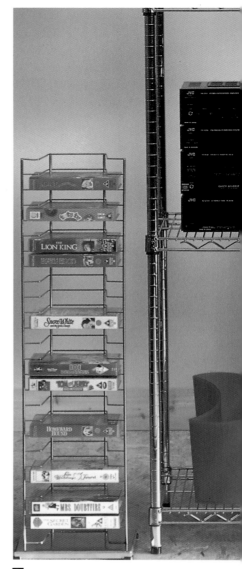

3

3 RACKS AND SHELVING

Media columns are an ideal way to keep your entertainment all in one place using vertical space.

4 DRESS ME UP

A brightly coloured portable storage unit is great for children's rooms.

5 MODULAR FURNITURE

Designed to fit into closets, these units utilize the wasted space beneath short hanging clothes.

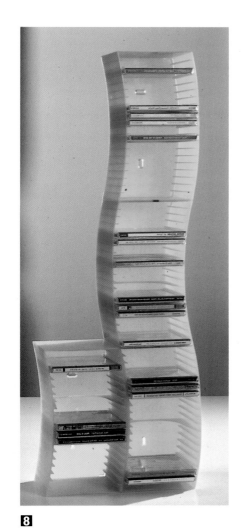

8

6

7

6 PERFECTLY ORDERED

Wavy plastic strips snap together to form 32 compartments neatly housing socks or underwear.

7 SHOE CUBBIES

A perfect way to stack shoes as high as you need, these are ideal for fitting under short hanging clothes or against a wall.

8 STORAGE WITH STYLE

Brightly coloured plastic CD holders stack to form a stylish, sculptural unit.

CONTAINERS

1 COTTON DISPENSER

A handy item which keeps this make-up essential ready to hand and tidy.

2 FABRIC STORAGE BAGS

Essential for travelling, fabric bags are ideal for separating shoes, jewellery and lingerie.

3 ALUMINIUM BOTTLES

Keep travel-size toiletries ready to go in aluminium bottles with pumps, sprays and twist tops.

1

SHOES

SWIMMING

2

3

4

5

6

7

8

9

10

4 AIRTIGHT STORAGE JARS

Colourful airtight jars can be used to store dry ingredients in the kitchen.

5 PLASTIC TROLLEY (CART)

A plastic trolley (cart) gives instant storage.

6 REINFORCED BOXES

Boxes are great under a bed or on top of shelves in a cupboard

7 STACKING CRATES

Build towers of see-through stackable storage – great for linen or clothing.

11

8 METAL BOXES

Use to store pens, paper and accessories.

9 ROUND CANISTERS

Metal canisters create an accessible cluster of everyday food items.

10 FOLDING PLASTIC CRATES

Strong and practical for heavy items such as books, these collapse when not needed.

11 MOBILE TOY CART

Provides three baskets to divide toys and keeps kids tidy.

CONTAINERS

12

16

13

14

14 WOVEN HAT BOXES

Protect fragile hats from crushing and dust with colourful hat boxes, which make an excellent design feature.

12 COLOURFUL STORAGE BOXES

Keep CDs, tapes and videos orderly with storage boxes available in a range of fashionable colours. Label by artist or alphabetically.

13 CARDBOARD CHESTS

Flat-packed cardboard furniture provides an inexpensive solution for storing excess or out-of-season gear, and can be customized by painting.

15

15 FABRIC-COVERED BOXES

Beautifully detailed boxes can be a design feature of any living area. Available in a variety of colours and sizes, they can be used to store clothing, papers or anything you fancy.

17

18

16 CHIC SHOPPER

Elevated to a fashion item, shopping trolleys make a come-back and save your back and arms in the process. The wheels pop up and the trolley folds up when empty.

17 ROLLING LAUNDRY HAMPERS

A wooden base on castors makes these laundry hampers a practical way in which to store dirty clothing.

18 ROLLING MAGAZINE RACKS

A clever way of storing magazines, these racks on castors allow the entire family to gain easy access. They are available in natural canvas and printed plastics.

STOCKISTS

Aero
96 Westbourne Grove
London
W2 5RT
0171 221 1950

B&Q
0800 600 900 for your nearest branch

The Conran Shop
Michelin House
81 Fulham Road
London
SW3 6RD
0171 589 7401

Habitat
0645 334433
for your nearest branch

Heal's
196 Tottenham Court Road
London
W1P 9LD
0171 636 1666

The Holding Company
243/245 King's Road
London
SW3 5EL
0171 352 1600

The Home
Salts Mill
Victoria Road
Saltaire
Bradford
BD18 3LB
01274 530770

Homebase
0645 801800 for your nearest branch

Ikea
0181 208 5600 for your nearest
branch

Lakeland Plastics
015394 88100 for mail-order details

Muji
39–41 Shelton Street
London
WC2H 9HJ
0171 379 1331

Muji
157 Kensington High Street
London
W8 6SU
0171 376 2484

Muji
77 King's Road
London
SW3 4NX
0171 352 7148

Muji
26 Great Marlborough Street
London
W1V 1HL
0171 494 1197

Peter Jones
Sloane Square
London
SW1V 8EL
0171 730 3434

0171 629 7711
for your nearest branch of the UK-
wide John Lewis partnership

AUSTRALIA

House & Garden of Burke
638 Burke Road
CAMBERWELL 3124
(03) 9882 0906

House & Garden of Brandon Park
Shop 111
Brandon Park Shopping Centre
Cnr Springvale and Ferntree
Gully Rds
MULGRAVE 3175
(03) 9561 8400

House & Garden of Highpoint
Shop 300
Level 3, Highpoint City
120–200 Rosamond Road
MARIBRYNONG 3032
(03) 9317 8134

House & Garden of Northland
Shop B24
Northland Shopping Centre
Murray Road
PRESTON 3072
(03) 9471 0222

House & Garden of Geelong
Shop 57, Gallery Level
Market Square
GEELONG 3220
(052) 23 2112

House & Garden of Shepparton
130 High Street
SHEPPARTON 3630
(058) 31 1767

House & Garden of Albury
490 Dean Street
ALBURY 2640
(060) 21 2311

House & Garden of Wagga Wagga
2/69 Bayliss Street
WAGGA WAGGA 2650
(069) 214 005

Mackay House & Garden
Shop 85/86
Caneland Shoppingtown
MACKAY 4740
(079) 57 2796

House & Garden of Bundaberg
Shop 20
Sugarland Shopping Centre
BUNDABERG
(071) 52 0577

House & Garden of Strathpine
Shop 66–67
Westfield Shoppingtown
STRATHPINE 4500
(07) 205 5351

House & Garden Pacific Fair
Shop 86
Pacific Fair
Hooker Blvd
BROADBEACH 4218
(075) 399 855

House & Garden of Sth Australia
Shop 35, Level 2
The Myer Centre
Rundle Mall
ADELAIDE 3000
(08) 8231 9988

Ikea Gordon
924 Pacific Highway
Gordon
NSW 2072
02 9498 3822

Ikea Blacktown
Homebase
19 Stoddart Road
Prospect
NSW 2149
02 9636 9222

Ikea Moore Park
Cnr South Dowling Street and
Todman Avenue
Moore Park
NSW 2021
02 9313 8140

IKEA Springwood
Cnr South East Fwy and Springwood
Road
Springwood
QLD 4127
07 3341 0000

IKEA Moorabbin
988 Nepean Hwy
Moorabbin
VIC 3189
03 9555 5222

IKEA Nunawading
274 Whitehorse Road
Nunawading
VIC 3131
03 9878 7999

IKEA Perth
405 Scarborough Beach Road
Osborne Park
WA 6017
09 242 6464

SOUTH AFRICA

Boardmans
Retail Stores
Shop 143
East Rand Mall, Boksburg
(011) 826 5151

Stuttafords Stores
Eastgate Shopping Centre
Bedford Road, Bedfordview
(011) 616 2045

The Rosebank Mall
50 Bath Avenue
Rosebank
(011) 788 1920

Sandton City
Rivonia Road, Sandton
(011) 783 5212

Westgate Shopping Mall
120 Ontdekkers Road
Roodeport
(011) 7681370

ACKNOWLEDGMENTS

1 Robin Matthews/Noname ; 4 Peter Mauss/Esto ; 5 above Jean-Marc Palisse ; 5 centre Ray Main ; 5 below Nicolas Tosi (J. Borgeaud)/Marie Claire Maison ; 6 -7 Alberto Piovano (Architect: Marco Romanelli)/Arcaid ; 10 -11 James Merrell/Options/Robert Harding Syndication ; 12 -13 Alberto Piovano (Architect: Krys Mys)/Arcaid ; 13 above & below Gilles de Chabaneix (D. Rozensztroch)/Marie Claire Maison ; 14 Nicolas Tosi (C. Ardouin)/Marie Claire Maison ; 15 Paul Ryan (Miki Astori)/International Interiors ; 16 -17 Gilles de Chabaneix (D.Rosensztroch)/Marie Claire Maison ; 17 above Nicolas Tosi (C. Ardouin)/Marie Claire Maison ; 17 below Neil Lorimer/Belle Magazine ; 18 -19 Richard Bryant (Architect: Gale & Prior)/Arcaid ; 20 -21 Richard Bryant (Courtesy of Hancock Shaker Village)/Arcaid ; 24 -25 Otto Polman/Ariadne ; 26-27 Gilles de Chabaneix (M. Kalt)/Marie Claire Maison ; 28 Simon Upton (Sue Skeen)/World of Interiors ; 29 Alexander Bailhache (C. Ardouin)/Marie Claire Maison ; 30-31 Henry Bourne/Elle Decoration ; 31 Nicolas Tosi (J. Borgeaud)/Marie Claire Maison ; 34 -35 Gilles de Chabaneix (D. Rozensztroch)/Marie Claire Maison ; 35 Alexander van Berge ; 36 Willem Rethmeier/Belle Magazine ; 36 -7 Jan Verlinde (Philip Simoen) ; 37 left Paul Ryan (Architect: Kobe & Ou)/International Interiors ; 37 right Earl Carter/Belle Magazine ; 38 above Fritz von der Schulenburg (Emily Todhunter)/The Interior Archive ; 38 below Chris Meads ; 39 left Simon Upton/Homes & Gardens/Robert Harding Syndication ; 39 right Paul Ryan(Robinson)/International Interiors ; 40 Hans Zeegers/Ariadne ; 41 above left Hans Zeegers/Ariadne ; 41 centre Paul Grootes/V.T.Wonen ; 41 above right Christopher Drake/Options/Robert Harding Syndication ; 42 left James Merrell/Options/Robert Harding Syndication; 42 right Polly Wreford/Homes & Gardens/Robert Harding Syndication; 42-43 Simon Upton/The World of Interiors; 46 -7 Paul Snow Courtesy of Australian House & Garden ; 48 -49 Earl Carter/Belle Magazine ; 49 right Peter Cook (Architects: Tugman Partnership); 49 above Chris Meads ; 50 Above Jean-Marc Palisse ; 50 below Huntley Hedworth/Elizabeth Whiting & Associates ; 51 Jean-Marc Palisse ; 52-3 Nadia Mackenzie (Alex Cox); 53 above Petrina Tinsley/Belle Magazine ; 53 below Paul Ryan (Miki Astori)/International Interiors ; 54 above Ray Main ; 54 below Ray Main ; 55 Eduardo Munoz/La Casa de Marie Claire ; 56 -57 Simon Brown (Clodagh Nolan)/The Interior Archive ; 58 above Greg Powlesland ; 58 below Simon Upton (Sue Skeen)/The World of Interiors ; 59 left Jan Verlinde (Pieter Vandenhout) ; 59 Above right Peter Cook (Stephen Bates); 59 below right Hotze Eisma/V.T.Wonen ; 60 above Janos Grapow ; 60 below Paul Warchol ; 61 left Simon Brown/The Interior Archive ; 61 above right Richard Davies ; 61 below right Francis Armand (J. Borgeaud)/Marie Claire Maison ; 62 above Ray Main ; 62 below Fritz von der Schulenburg (Paola Navone)/The Interior Archive ; 62 -3 Peter Cook (Architect:Tugman Partnership); 64 above left Jean-Marc Palisse ; 64 below left Simon Brown (Justin Meath Baker)/The Interior Archive ; 64 -5 Paul Ryan (Miki Astori)/International Interiors ; 66 Robin Matthews/Noname ; 66 -7 Earl Carter/Belle Magazine ; 67 below left Ray Main ; 67 below right Christopher Drake/Options/Robert Harding Syndication ; 68 Johnathon Pilkington/The Interior Archive ; 68 -9 Barbara Rix (C.Ardouin)/Marie Claire Maison ; 69 Tom Leighton/Options/Robert Harding Syndication ; 70 Ray Main ; 71 above Verne Fotografie (Ralf Coussee & Klaas Goris); 71 below Paul Ryan(David Ling)/International Interiors ; 72-3 Hotze Eisma/V.T.Wonen ; 73 above & below Peter Cook (Architects:Tugman Partnership); 74 -5 Wayne Vincent (Lee Mallett)/The Interior Archive ; 76 Nick Pope/Options/Robert Harding Syndication ; 76 -7 Verne Fotografie (Jan Vandendorpe); 77 Petrina Tinsley/Belle Magazine ; 78 Jean-Marc Palisse ; 79 Jean-Marc Palisse/Madame Figaro ; 80 -1 Ray Main ; 81 above Gilles de Chabaneix (D. Rosensztroch)/Marie Claire Maison ; 81 centre Willem Rethmeier/Belle Magazine ; 81 below Christopher Drake/Options/Robert Harding Syndication ; 82 Ted Yarwood ; 83 above James Mortimer (Wendy Harrop)/The Interior Archive ; 83 centre Paul Ryan (J.M. Ekelblad)/International Interiors ; 83 below left Jean-Marc Palisse/Madame Figaro ; 83 below right Jean-Marc Palisse ; 84 -85 Wayne Vincent (Lee Mallett)/The Interior Archive ; 86 -7 Witney Cox (Architect: Anthony Plesko); 87 above Henry Wilson (Anand Zenz)/The Interior Archive ; 87 below Verne Fotografie (Vincent van Duyssen); 88 Paul Ryan(Chermayeff) /International Interiors ; 88 -9 Fritz von

der Schulenburg (Andrew Wadsworth)/The Interior Archive ; 89 Fritz von der Schulenburg (Jorg Marguard)/The Interior Archive ; 90 -1 Tim Beddow/World of Interiors ; 92 Witney Cox (Architect: Abels & Sherrerd); 92-93 Willem Rethmeier/Belle Magazine ; 93 above Jennifer Levy ; 93 below Fritz von der Schulenburg (Andre de Carceray)/The Interior Archive ; 94 Verne Fotografie (Waww); 95 Nadia Mackenzie (Alex Cox); 96 -7 Peter Mauss/Esto ; 97 above Jonathon Pilkington/The Interior Archive ; 97 below Jonathon Pilkington/The Interior Archive ; 98 James Mortimer (Wendy Harrop)/The Interior Archive ; 99 above Trevor Richards/Abode ; 99 centre James Merrell/Options/Robert Harding Syndication ; 99 below Christopher Drake/Options/Robert Harding Syndication ; 100 left James Merrell/Options/Robert Harding Syndication ; 100 right Paul Warchol ; 101 left Ray Main ; 101 above right James Merrell/Options/Robert Harding Syndication ; 101 below right James Merrell/Options/Robert Harding Syndication ; 102 -3 Verne Fotografie (Domus); 103 above Simon Brown/The Interior Archive ; 103 centre Hans Zeegers/Ariadne ; 103 below Otto Polman/Ariadne ; 104 -5 Fritz von der Schulenburg (Diane Berger)/The Interior Archive ; 105 Ray Main ; 106 -7 Fritz von der Schulenburg (Nico Rensch)/The Interior Archive ; 108 above Jan Baldwin/Options/Robert Harding Syndication ; 108 below Hans Zeegers/Ariadne ; 109 Elizabeth Zeschin/World of Interiors; 110 above Paul Ryan(Caroline Breet)/ International Interiors ; 110 below Philippe Costes (C.

Puech)/Marie Claire Maison ; 111 Verne Fotografie (Vincent Van Duysen); 112 above Gilles de Chabaneix (D.Rozenstroch)/Marie Claire Maison ; 112 below Andreas von Einsiedel/Elizabeth Whiting & Associates ; 113 Brigitte/ Camera Press ; 114 above Tom Leighton/Options/Robert Harding Syndication ; 114 below Suzanna Clarke Courtesy of Australian House & Garden ; 115 above Paul Warchol ; 115 below Otto Polman/Ariadne ; 116 -117 Rodney Hyett/Elizabeth Whiting & Associates ; 118 Wayne Vincent (Lesley Saddington)/The Interior Archive ; 119 above Henry Wilson (Jenny Romyn)/The Interior Archive ; 119 below Hans Zeegers/Ariadne ; 120 -121 Schoner Wohnen/Camera Press ; 121 above Otto Polman/Ariadne ; 121 below Dook/House & Leisure ; 122 -123 Fritz von der Schulenburg (Emily Todhunter)/The Interior Archive ; 123 above Eric Victor-Perdraut Courtesy of Australian House & Garden ; 123 centre Rodney Hyett/Elizabeth Whiting & Associates ; 123 below Nick Carter/Elizabeth Whiting & Associates ; 124 -125 Dennis Brandsma/V.T. Wonen ; 126 Fritz von der Schulenburg/The Interior Archive ; 127 Dennis Gilbert/Arcaid ; 128 -129 Michel Claus ; 129 Christoph Kicherer/Elle Decoration ; 130 -131 Dennis Brandsma/V.T. Wonen ; 131 above Gilles de Chabaneix(D. Rozensztroch)/Marie Claire Maison ; 131 below Jennifer Levy ; 132 Richard Davies ; 133 left Nicolas Tosi (C.Ardouin)/Marie Claire Maison ; 133 above right Jerome Darblay/Stock Image Production ; 133 below right Jennifer Levy ; 134 Nicolas Tosi (J. Borgeaud)/Marie Claire Maison ; 135 left Elizabeth Whiting & Associates ;

135 right Greg Powlesland ; 136 -137 Solvi Dos Santos ; 137 Hugh Palmer ; 138 -139 Mark Darley/Esto ; 140 Wayne Vincent (Roger Oates)/The Interior Archive ; 141 Paul Warchol ; 142 James Mortimer/The Interior Archive ; 142 -143 Dolf Straatemeir/V.T. Wonen ; 143 Alberto Piovano (Architect:Mariano Boggia)/ Arcaid; 146 above left Christpher Drake/Options/Robert Harding Syndication ; 146 below left Simon Upton/Homes & Gardens/Robert Harding Syndication ; 146 -149 Tom Graty/The Holding Company; 150 above Steve Dalton & Sue Pitman/The Holding Company ; 150 below left & right Simon Upton/Homes & Gardens/Robert Harding Syndication ; 151 above left Muji ; 151 above right & centre right Simon Upton/Homes & Gardens/Robert Harding Syndication ; 151 centre Muji ; 151 below Tom Graty/The Holding Company 152 - 153 Tom Graty/The Holding Company.

Author's Acknowledgments

There are numerous people who have inspired me along the way to make *Organized Living* a reality. First and foremost, Helen Chislett, who spent countless hours listening to me extol the virtues of organized living and managed to capture in words all of the emotion. Sue Pitman and Steve Dalton who have shown in pictures that storage can be stylish. Judy at Camron who from The Holding Company's inception — got it and continues to be a sounding board for our future plans. Last but not least, to the staff of The Holding Company who delight me every day with their unbridled enthusiasm for helping to simplify our customers' lives.